PRAYERSCRIPTS

30 DAYS OF PRAYERS AND DECLARATIONS TO
SECURE YOUR REST & SHAPE YOUR TOMORROW

CYRIL OPOKU

Command Your Night: *30 Days of Prayers and Declarations to Secure Your Rest and Shape Your Tomorrow*

© 2025 Cyril Opoku. *PrayerScripts*. All rights reserved.

No part of this publication may be reproduced, stored in a retrieval system, or transmitted in any form or by any means—electronic, mechanical, photocopy, recording, or otherwise—without the prior written permission of the publisher, except in the case of brief quotations used in reviews, articles, or devotionals.

Published by *Quest Publications*

ISBN: 978-1-988439-65-5

Cover design by *Quest Publications (questpublications@outlook.com)*

Unless otherwise indicated, all Scripture quotations are taken from the World English Bible (WEB), which is in the public domain. For more information, visit: www.worldenglish.bible

This book is a work of devotional encouragement. It is not intended to replace biblical study, pastoral counsel, or professional therapy.

Printed in the United States of America.

First Edition: July 2025

For more books like this, visit *PrayerScripts:* *https://prayerscripts.org*

Contents

Contents .... *iii*
Preface .... *x*
Introduction .... *xii*
How to Use This Book .... *xiv*

DAY 1 1
Shutting the Gates of Harm 1
Covered by Wings of Mercy 2
Be Still, O Voices 3
Speak, Lord, In the Night 4
I Lie Down in Victory 5

DAY 2 7
Boundaries the Enemy Cannot Cross 7
My Glory and My Covering 8
The Lord Will Fight for Me 9
Dreams Poured Out Like Rain 10
Sweet Rest for My Soul 11

DAY 3 12
Doors the Enemy Cannot Open 12
Favor Is My Surrounding Shield 13
Peace, Be Still in Me 14
Night Counsel from Heaven 15
Perfect Peace in My Mind 16

DAY 4 17
Lift the Gates and Lock Them 17
Shielded by Every Word 18
He Sings While I Sleep 19

Light in the Night Season..20
He Gives While I Rest...21

DAY 5 22
Chains Broken, Gates Closed 22
Faithful to Guard My Night 23
No Weapon Will Speak Tonight 24
He Speaks While I Sleep...25
Rest that Revives My Spirit 26

DAY 6 27
The Destroyer Must Pass Over 27
My Rock and Fortress..28
Hidden from the Strife of Tongues 29
Secrets Shared in Stillness 30
Rest in the Land of Promise...31

DAY 7 32
A Wall of Fire Around Me 32
My Strength, My Shield, My Song...33
I Will Wait in Praise...34
In All My Ways, Guide Me..35
You Satisfy My Soul with Rest 36

DAY 8 37
The Devourer Is Rebuked 37
Help from His Holy Heaven 38
Fear Has No Voice Here..39
The Kingdom Is Mine to Receive 40
Come to Me and Rest..41

DAY 9 42
Surrounded Like Mount Zion 42
Nothing Withheld from the Upright 43
Hidden in His Pavilion 44
Revelation in the Night 45
Soaring in My Stillness 46

DAY 10 47
You Drew Near and Defended Me 47
You Lifted Me Up 48
The God of Peace Will Crush 49
Open My Eyes to Wonder 50
He Leads Me Beside Still Waters 51

DAY 11 52
When the Enemy Rushes In 52
Covered in Battle and Still 53
Peace Be Still 54
Wisdom in the Night Watches 55
Enter the Sabbath of His Rest 56

DAY 12 57
Hide Me in the Shadow 57
My Fortress, My Deliverer 58
Tread on Serpents in Peace 59
Led by the Eye of God 60
Life, Peace, and Holy Rest 61

DAY 13 62
Preserved From All Evil 62
Flawless Shield of My God 63
Though I Fall, I Rise 64

  Your Voice Behind Me 65
  Return to Rest, O My Soul 66

DAY 14 67
  The Name That Seals Me 67
  Held by His Hand 68
  Peace in My Inner Storm 69
  Led by the Spirit of Truth 70
  Dwelling in the Secret Place 71

DAY 15 72
  Encamped by Heaven's Host 72
  Unshakable and Unmoved 73
  The Enemy Has Been Disarmed 74
  A Door Standing Open in Heaven 75
  After You Have Suffered a While 76

DAY 16 77
  Make the Crooked Places Straight 77
  A Stronghold in the Day of Trouble 78
  Peace That Guards My Mind 79
  I Will Speak in Visions 80
  Songs in the Night 81

DAY 17 82
  You Are My Hiding Place 82
  Flawless Defender of My Way 83
  He Will Bless Me With Peace 84
  I Will Stand and Watch 85
  I Lay Down and Slept 86

DAY 18 87
Preserved From the Hands of the Wicked 87
Angels on Assignment 88
Why Are You Afraid? 89
Dreams and Visions in the Night 90
I Will Heal You in Rest 91

DAY 19 92
They Shall Not Prevail 92
Underneath Are Everlasting Arms 93
Take Every Thought Captive 94
In Your Light, I See Light 95
The Keeper Who Never Sleeps 96

DAY 20 97
Whom Shall I Fear? 97
The Lord Is My Strength 98
Redeemed From the Battle 99
You Reveal Deep Things 100
Held by His Embrace 101

DAY 21 102
The Heavens Fight for Me 102
Rescued and Surrounded 103
Keys to Lock and Loose 104
Speak, Lord—I'm Listening 105
Remembering You in the Night 106

DAY 22 107
Hidden in the Shelter 107
The Cry of the Oppressed 108
You Still the Roaring 109

    Steps Directed by the Lord 110
    Watered in the Wilderness 111

DAY 23 112
    The Breaker Has Gone Before 112
    Singing Through the Night 113
    Be Silent, and Come Out 114
    He Made Known His Ways 115
    Faithfulness in the Night 116

DAY 24 117
    The Name That Defends Me 117
    Our Soul Waits for the Lord 118
    Above All, Take the Shield 119
    Revealing the Hidden Mysteries 120
    You Are With Me in the Waters 121

DAY 25 122
    No Chaos, No Chase 122
    Your Gentleness Makes Me Great 123
    My Soul Is Quieted 124
    Eyes Open in the Night 125
    Tomorrow Will Worry for Itself 126

DAY 26 127
    Refuge in the Midst of Trouble 127
    Unshakable Confidence 128
    No Wisdom Can Prevail 129
    Taught by the Spirit 130
    Darkness Is Not Dark to You 131

DAY 27 132
   Affliction Shall Not Rise Again 132
   You Are My Strong Tower 133
   By the Blood and My Testimony 134
   Wisdom, Knowledge, and Understanding 135
   The Lord Sustains the Weary 136

DAY 28 137
   My Refuge in Times of Trouble 137
   I Love You, O Lord, My Strength 138
   Quietness and Trust Will Be My Strength 139
   You Will Seek Me and Find Me 140
   He Will Quiet Me With His Love 141

DAY 29 142
   Open Only the Gates of Righteousness 142
   Let Your Mercy Always Surround Me 143
   The Lord Reigns —Let Every Other Voice Be Still 144
   Light for the Next Step 145
   Abounding in Hope and Rest 146

DAY 30 147
   Preserve Me, O God 147
   I Will Trust and Not Be Afraid 148
   With a Sword in My Mouth 149
   The Spirit of Prophecy Is Jesus 150
   There Shall Be No Night There 151

   Epilogue *152*
   Encourage Others with Your Story *153*
   More from PrayerScripts *154*

Preface

"I will both lie down in peace, and sleep; for You alone, O Lord, make me dwell in safety." —Psalm 4:8

There is a battle over every night, just as there is over every morning. While the day is often filled with noise, activity, and visibility, the night carries its own quiet warfare—unseen, unspoken, but deeply spiritual. In the stillness, voices rise. In the dark, strategies are formed. And for many, the night has become a time of fear, anxiety, torment, and vulnerability.

But Scripture paints a different picture for the believer. The night is not meant to master us—we are meant to command it. Psalm 4:8 reminds us that sleep is not merely physical—it is spiritual. Peace is not circumstantial—it is covenantal. Safety is not the absence of threat—it is the presence of God.

This prayer devotional is the night companion to *Command Your Morning*. Where that volume helps you seize your day, *Command Your Night* equips you to secure your rest, silence the adversary, and set your spirit in alignment with God before sleep. Each night includes five prophetic prayer themes—**Shut, Shield, Silence, Show,** and **Sleep**—each rooted in Scripture and designed to help you reclaim the night season as holy ground.

As you begin this 30-day journey, may the Lord train your hands for warfare and your soul for rest. May your nights become altars of peace, wells of revelation, and thresholds of breakthrough.

Sleep will no longer be where battles chase you. It will be where victory finds you. In Jesus' name, Amen.

In Christ's authority,
Cyril O.
Illinois, July 2025

Introduction

Every night is a spiritual battlefield—what you do before you sleep can determine the course of your tomorrow.

Command Your Night is your weapon and your shield, empowering you to take authority over the darkness, silence the enemy's schemes, and secure the rest that fuels your destiny. It is designed to help you take spiritual authority over your nights, transforming them into times of divine peace, protection, and prophetic preparation. Just as *Command Your Morning* helps you seize the day with purpose, *Command Your Night* prayer devotional guides you to close each evening with bold prayers and prophetic declarations grounded in Scripture.

The night is not merely a time to rest—it's a sacred season to **shut** the gates of darkness, invoking a divine sealing over your life, mind, and home from all nocturnal attacks. It is a time to **shield** yourself under His wings, calling on the protective covering of God's presence to surround and defend you. It is a time to **silence** every midnight voice—those tormenting thoughts, accusations, and satanic whispers that often try to rob you of peace and clarity. It is a time to cry out, "**Show** me Your ways, O Lord," and invite divine revelation, dreams, and instruction in the night watches. And finally, it is a time to declare in faith: "I lie down and **sleep** in victory," believing that your rest is not passive but filled with recovery, renewal, and resurrection strength for the morning ahead.

Over the next 30 days, you'll learn to command your nights with intentional faith, protecting your soul and preparing your spirit for all that God has in store. By mastering your nights, you lay a firm foundation for a powerful tomorrow.

Let this prayer devotional be your guide to approaching each evening with confidence and expectancy, knowing that God's presence will guard your sleep and renew your strength. Rest deeply. Rise strong. Command your night!

How to Use This Book

Command Your Night is a 30-day journey designed to help you close each day in spiritual authority and peace. Each nightly devotional leads you into prophetic prayer through **five distinct themes,** each anchored in Scripture and crafted to equip you for rest that is both protected and powerful.

Here's how the nightly framework unfolds:

- **Shut – Shut the Gates of Darkness:** A divine sealing of your life, mind, and home from all nocturnal attacks.
- **Shield – Cover Me with Your Wings:** A night covering by God's presence; invoking His protective shield.
- **Silence – Silence Every Midnight Voice:** Command the hush of tormenting thoughts, accusations, and satanic whispers.
- **Show – Visit Me in the Night Watches:** A cry for divine dreams, revelation, and instruction—"Show me Your ways, O Lord."
- **Sleep – I Lie Down and Sleep in Victory:** A prophetic declaration of rest, recovery, and resurrection strength by morning.

Each day begins with five handpicked Scriptures—one for each theme—followed by five prophetic prayer scripts, written in the first person to help you boldly declare God's Word over your night.

To make the most of your journey:

1. **Set aside time each evening,** ideally just before bed, to quiet your heart and focus on God.

2. **Read the Scriptures,** allowing them to renew your mind and prepare your spirit.
3. **Pray through each themed section,** slowly and intentionally, declaring each word with faith.
4. **Personalize the prayers**—insert names, situations, or anything the Holy Spirit brings to mind.
5. **Lie down with expectation,** knowing God watches over His Word to perform it—even in your sleep.

This is more than a devotional—it is a nightly altar, a place to end your day in power, shut every gate to the enemy, and rise the next morning in victory.

Your night is not a time of retreat—it is a time of divine covering, revelation, and renewal.

Command it well.

DAY 1

SHUT

SHUTTING THE GATES OF HARM

> Come, my people, enter into your rooms, and shut your doors behind you. Hide yourself for a little moment, until the indignation is past. For, behold, Yahweh comes out of his place to punish the inhabitants of the earth for their iniquity. The earth also will disclose her blood, and will no longer cover her slain.
> —Isaiah 26:20-21 WEB

Father, I come into this night with holy authority. In the name of Jesus, I shut every spiritual gate that the enemy would attempt to exploit. I close every access point that would allow torment, fear, or destruction to enter. I declare that no weapon formed against me shall prosper tonight. No darkness will encroach upon the borders You have established. Just as You sealed Noah in the ark before the floods came, seal me tonight in Your divine protection.

I close the gates of my mind to anxiety, nightmares, and mental warfare. I close the gates of my emotions to fear, shame, and regret. I shut the door to every demonic cycle, every spiritual ambush, and every assignment of the enemy meant to destabilize me while I sleep. Lord, stand at the threshold of my home and forbid entry to anything not sent by You. Let every agent of evil be turned away in confusion and defeat.

Tonight, I rest behind the blood. I am hidden in Christ. My home is under lock and seal by the Word of God. As judgment moves in the earth, I am preserved in Your mercy. My atmosphere is guarded. My night is sanctified.

In Jesus' name, Amen.

SHIELD

COVERED BY WINGS OF MERCY

> He will cover you with his feathers. Under his wings you will take refuge. His faithfulness is your shield and rampart.
> —Psalms 91:4 WEB

Almighty God, tonight I step under the canopy of Your protection. You are my shield and defense, and in You I trust. As the night settles, I declare that I am not vulnerable, for I am covered by the wings of the Almighty. Let every invisible threat be intercepted by Your mighty hand. Let every flaming arrow be extinguished by the shield of Your truth.

Wrap me in Your feathers, and let no harm come near my dwelling. I refuse to sleep in fear or uncertainty. I place every part of my life—body, soul, and spirit—under Your watchful eye. You neither slumber nor sleep. While I rest, You war for me. Let angels be stationed at every corner of my home, every bedpost, every boundary line. Let their flaming swords drive out every demonic presence.

Shield my heart from heaviness. Shield my mind from intrusive thoughts. Shield my body from sickness and restlessness. Surround me with Your faithfulness like a wall of fire. Let Your presence press against every threat until peace reigns in my home. Let the enemy pass over me, unable to penetrate the covering You provide.

Tonight, I am safe—not by might, not by strength, but by the shelter of my God.

In Jesus' name, Amen.

SILENCE

BE STILL, O VOICES

> "Be still, and know that I am God. I will be exalted among the nations. I will be exalted in the earth."
> —Psalms 46:10 WEB

O Lord my God, tonight I silence every voice that dares rise against the knowledge of who You are in my life. I take authority over the night and command every lying whisper, every condemning thought, every tormenting spirit to be still. I reject every voice that is not aligned with the voice of my Shepherd. I cast down imaginations, mute the noise of fear, and declare: I will hear only what heaven is saying over me.

Let the winds and waves of anxiety obey Your command. Let every internal storm submit to Your peace. The voices of failure, of past shame, of future uncertainty have no place in the sanctuary of my soul. You are enthroned in my heart, and no intruder has legal right to speak here. I declare my mind a guarded gate, sanctified by the Word of God and the blood of Jesus.

Even now, Lord, let Your voice rise louder within me. Drown out the enemy with the sound of Your nearness. Whisper peace, declare truth, sing over me with songs of deliverance. I rest, not just in silence, but in the sound of Your assurance.

Be still, O soul. God is here. I will not be moved.

In Jesus' name, Amen.

Show

Speak, Lord, In the Night

> 'Call to me, and I will answer you, and will show you great and difficult things, which you don't know.'
> —Jeremiah 33:3 WEB

Lord, my heart is open tonight. Speak to me in ways only You can. As I quiet myself and lay down, I invite Your voice to enter the depths of my spirit. Reveal the secrets of heaven. Illuminate the path ahead. Let this night not pass without Your instruction, Your comfort, and Your correction. I don't want to sleep just to escape the day—I want to sleep to encounter You.

Remove the clutter of my thoughts so I can hear You clearly. Cancel out the noise of the world and let divine revelation break through. I ask for dreams that carry Your truth, visions that sharpen my discernment, and whispers that lead me into deeper intimacy with You. Unveil strategies, uncover hidden dangers, unlock prophetic direction.

Lord, You promised to show great and mighty things I do not know. So, tonight, I yield my mind to divine visitation. Whether in visions or gentle impressions, speak. I am listening, even in sleep. I ask for supernatural clarity, fresh insight, and holy conviction. Lead me by Your Spirit through the night watches.

Let this be a night of encounter, where heaven touches earth and I awaken with understanding.

In Jesus' name, Amen.

SLEEP

I LIE DOWN IN VICTORY

> In peace I will both lay myself down and sleep, for you, Yahweh alone, make me live in safety.
> —Psalms 4:8 WEB

Father, I come to the end of this day with gratitude and authority. I declare that this night shall not be stolen from me by fear, anxiety, or spiritual interference. I will lie down and sleep, not in defeat, but in victory. My battles are in Your hands. My future is secure in You. I release every burden, every unanswered question, every lingering concern—I place it all at Your feet.

Tonight, my bed becomes an altar. I surrender my body for restoration and my spirit for renewal. Let peace saturate every muscle, let calm flow through every heartbeat. I am not bracing for the next attack—I am resting in the triumph of my God. You have fought for me, and now I lie down under the banner of victory.

Let healing flow as I rest. Let dreams of hope and strength arise. Let Your Spirit breathe over me until morning. I will not wake in panic—I will rise in praise. I rest not because I am weak, but because You are strong. And while I sleep, You watch. You war. You win.

Sleep is not escape—it is worship, it is trust, it is warfare on heaven's terms.

In Jesus' name, Amen.

DAY 2

SHUT

BOUNDARIES THE ENEMY CANNOT CROSS

> "Or who shut up the sea with doors, when it broke out of the womb, when I made clouds its garment, and wrapped it in thick darkness, marked out for it my bound, set bars and doors, and said, 'Here you may come, but no further. Here your proud waves shall be stayed?'
> —Job 38:8-11 WEB

Almighty God, I rise tonight in spiritual authority and declare: the boundaries around my life are established by Your hand, and no darkness can cross them. You are the One who assigned limits to the sea and said, "This far you may come and no farther." In the same way, I decree that every wave of chaos, every storm of fear, every flood of oppression is halted by Your divine command.

Tonight, I enforce Your decree over my life. I shut the gates of torment and seal off every breach where the enemy would try to infiltrate my thoughts, my family, or my rest. No curse will cross the bloodline. No accusation will cross the truth of Your Word. No demonic assignment will breach the wall of fire that surrounds me. I raise the banner of the Lord and declare my home a fortress of peace.

Let angels stand as sentinels at every corner of my dwelling. Let the enemy be pushed back, unable to pass the lines You have drawn. I live inside the Word, inside the promise, inside the boundaries of grace—and here, no harm can find me.

In Jesus' name, Amen.

SHIELD

MY GLORY AND MY COVERING

> But you, Yahweh, are a shield around me, my glory, and the one who lifts up my head.
> —Psalms 3:3 WEB

Lord, You are a shield around me—my glory and the One who lifts my head. I come into this night not uncovered, not exposed, but surrounded by Your presence. While the world sleeps unaware, I rest in the knowledge that You are actively defending me. You go before me as fire, and You stand behind me as protection. Every side of my life is enclosed in Your goodness.

Even when the enemy surrounds me, I will not fear. You lift my head above fear, above shame, above the noise of the enemy. You are not just my protection—you are my honor. I will not bow to worry or dread, because I know whose shield covers me. I declare that no weapon formed against me will prosper. No fiery dart will find its mark. No spiritual ambush will surprise me.

Tonight, I lay down in the covering of Your majesty. Let angels guard my gate. Let peace be my portion. Let every spiritual attack crumble before it reaches my camp. My sleep is not exposed—my sleep is enveloped in the shield of the Most High. In Jesus' name, Amen.

Silence

The Lord Will Fight for Me

> Yahweh will fight for you, and you shall be still."
> —Exodus 14:14 WEB

Tonight, I choose stillness—not the stillness of defeat, but the stillness of confidence. You, O Lord, are my Defender, and I do not need to strive in the night. Every voice that would stir fear, every whisper of worry, every suggestion of despair—I command it to be silenced. I do not need to fight the thoughts that rise against me; I simply stand still and watch my God go before me.

You fight for me while I sleep. You battle in realms I cannot see. You silence the accuser and break the power of every demonic voice that seeks to disturb my rest. The enemy may try to wage war in the night, but I am not afraid. The Lord is in the camp. The sound of the Lord's voice is greater than any whisper of fear.

Let the raging noise of the enemy be drowned in Your stillness. Let every tormenting spirit be muzzled by the presence of God. I will not be moved. I will not be shaken. I rest tonight in the assurance that the Lord has taken up my cause and I shall see the victory.

In Jesus' name, Amen.

SHOW

DREAMS POURED OUT LIKE RAIN

"It will happen afterward, that I will pour out my Spirit on all flesh; and your sons and your daughters will prophesy. Your old men will dream dreams. Your young men will see visions.
—Joel 2:28 WEB

Father, I thank You that the night hours are not empty—they are sacred. I stand under open heavens tonight and ask that You pour out dreams, visions, and divine impressions like rain upon my spirit. You promised to pour out Your Spirit on all flesh, and I receive that promise now. Let Your voice be made known to me in dreams. Let divine mysteries be revealed in the stillness of the night.

I open the gates of my soul to receive heavenly instruction. I will not sleep aimlessly—I will sleep expectantly. Let my dreams be filled with insight, warning, direction, and encouragement. May visions come with clarity, and impressions with wisdom. Let me wake with purpose because of what You deposit in the night.

Silence the noise so I can hear You clearly. Remove confusion so I can interpret what You reveal. Speak to me like You did to Joseph, to Daniel, to Samuel. Let me be one who receives revelation when the world is asleep. I surrender my sleep to You and ask for divine encounter.

In Jesus' name, Amen.

Sleep

Sweet Rest for My Soul

> When you lie down, you will not be afraid. Yes, you will lie down, and your sleep will be sweet.
> —Proverbs 3:24 WEB

Tonight, I will lie down without fear. I will rest deeply, securely, and sweetly, for Your Word declares that when I lie down, my sleep will be sweet. I release every anxiety, every leftover thought from the day. I choose to trust You more than I trust my plans or problems. My bed is not just a place of rest—it is an altar of surrender.

I cast my burdens on You, Lord, because You care for me. I do not toss and turn in fear of tomorrow. I do not replay the failures of the day. I yield my body to restoration and my spirit to communion with You. Let every part of me be renewed in this holy rest. Let healing visit me in sleep. Let strength rise up as I dream. Let my rest be unshaken, my room be filled with Your peace.

You give Your beloved sleep—and I am Your beloved. I rest tonight not because everything is perfect, but because You are perfectly faithful. Let the night hours restore what life tried to drain. I will wake up refreshed, refilled, and ready to walk in purpose.

In Jesus' name, Amen.

DAY 3

SHUT

DOORS THE ENEMY CANNOT OPEN

> "To the angel of the assembly in Philadelphia write: "He who is holy, he who is true, he who has the key of David, he who opens and no one can shut, and who shuts and no one opens, says these things: "I know your works (behold, I have set before you an open door, which no one can shut), that you have a little power, and kept my word, and didn't deny my name.
> —Revelation 3:7-8 WEB

Father, tonight I stand in the authority of the One who holds the key of David—who opens and no one shuts, and shuts and no one opens. You have set before me an open door that no man, no demon, and no circumstance can close. And You have also shut doors that no force of darkness can reopen. I agree with heaven tonight: every entry point the enemy once used is now sealed by divine decree.

I shut the gates of fear, oppression, confusion, and sabotage. I shut doors to relationships that You have ended, to patterns that led to defeat, and to past sins that no longer have a claim on me. I declare that every demonic corridor is closed, every spiritual loophole is sealed, and every doorway not authorized by You is now guarded by angelic sentinels.

You are the doorkeeper of my life. I trust You to close what must be closed, and to secure what must remain locked. The enemy cannot hijack my night or trespass on my peace. The blood of Jesus marks my threshold. My dwelling is sealed with promise, and I lie down in the safety of Your divine boundaries.

In Jesus' name, Amen.

SHIELD

FAVOR IS MY SURROUNDING SHIELD

> For you will bless the righteous. Yahweh, you will surround him with favor as with a shield.
> —Psalms 5:12 WEB

O Lord, You bless the righteous, and You surround them with favor as with a shield. I stand tonight clothed in the righteousness of Christ, not by my own merit, but by the covering of the cross. Because of that, I am wrapped in divine favor—shielded, surrounded, and safe from harm. While others lie vulnerable, I lie in the encampment of grace.

Let Your favor surround my body—let sickness and weariness pass over. Surround my mind—let torment and dread find no place. Surround my atmosphere—let every plan of the enemy dissolve on contact with Your favor. I am not merely defended—I am favored. Your love stands like armor, and Your pleasure is a wall of protection around me.

Tonight, I do not just survive—I am embraced by the delight of my God. Where the enemy expected to find me open and afraid, he finds me hidden in favor, covered in blessing. Let no weapon prosper. Let no lie take root. Let every attack collapse at the edge of Your presence. I sleep in the safety of a shield that never fails. In Jesus' name, Amen.

SILENCE

PEACE, BE STILL IN ME

> He awoke, and rebuked the wind, and said to the sea, "Peace! Be still!" The wind ceased, and there was a great calm.
> —Mark 4:39 WEB

Tonight, I command the storm to cease. Every whirlwind of anxiety, every wave of fear, every loud and violent thought—I speak to you now as my Savior did to the sea: peace, be still. You have no authority in my atmosphere. The Prince of Peace is in the boat with me, and I will not sink beneath this storm.

I silence the voices that replay old trauma, ignite panic, or stir doubt. I do not negotiate with torment. I do not debate with lies. I lift up the name of Jesus and release peace into the chaos. Let the winds cease. Let the waves lay down. Let my soul, once unsettled, now be anchored in the calm of Your Word.

This is not just emotional quiet—it is divine stillness. It is spiritual peace, wrapped in power. I declare that tonight, nothing will disrupt the deep rest of a soul protected by Christ. No nightmare, no fear, no inner war will rise again. The voice of Jesus rules the night, and every storm must obey.

In Jesus' name, Amen.

SHOW

NIGHT COUNSEL FROM HEAVEN

> I will bless Yahweh, who has given me counsel. Yes, my heart instructs me in the night seasons.
> —Psalms 16:7 WEB

Lord, I bless You tonight for You instruct my heart even in the night seasons. As I prepare to sleep, I invite Your counsel to surround me. Speak to me in dreams, correct me in visions, and guide me with Your still, small voice. I do not lie down just to recover—I lie down to receive. The night belongs to You, and so does every hour of my rest.

Let the darkness be filled with divine light. Let the thoughts You plant in my spirit grow into wisdom by morning. I open the ears of my heart to Your whispers. As I lay down, I position myself to be taught. Speak to me about what's ahead. Warn me about unseen dangers. Remind me of what You've promised.

I welcome instruction that is drenched in love and rich with clarity. You do not sleep, and while I do, You continue to lead. Thank You for being the God who speaks even in silence, who teaches while I rest, and who prepares me in the night for victories in the morning.

In Jesus' name, Amen.

SLEEP

Perfect Peace in My Mind

> You will keep whoever's mind is steadfast in perfect peace, because he trusts in you.
> —Isaiah 26:3 WEB

Tonight, I receive the peace that passes understanding—not the fragile calm the world offers, but the steady, unshakable peace that flows from trust in You. You will keep in perfect peace the one whose mind is stayed on You, and that one is me. I fix my thoughts on You now. I turn away from worry. I cast off distractions. I let go of control. My mind rests in the truth of who You are.

There is no fear here. No dread, no turmoil. Just You—present, powerful, and near. I release the day and embrace the stillness of knowing that You are in control. My sleep is not delayed by anxiety or disturbed by confusion. It is guarded by the God of peace, who surrounds me with Himself.

Let this night be a sanctuary of serenity. Let my dreams be soaked in Your goodness. Let my breath slow, my body soften, my spirit rise in gratitude. I will lie down and sleep in perfect peace because You, Lord, are the keeper of my mind.

You are my anchor. You are my rest.

In Jesus' name, Amen.

DAY 4

SHUT

LIFT THE GATES AND LOCK THEM

> Lift up your heads, you gates; yes, lift them up, you everlasting doors, and the King of glory will come in. Who is this King of glory? Yahweh of Armies is the King of glory! Selah.
> —Psalms 24:9-10 WEB

King of Glory, tonight I lift up the gates of my life to You. Come in with power. Enter in with fire. Take full possession of my night and every threshold that leads to my soul. I welcome Your rule, and at the same time, I command every unauthorized gate to be closed and sealed by the blood of Jesus. Let every demonic access point be exposed and barred. No spirit not sent by You has the right to cross into this holy dwelling.

Let ancient doors of fear, compromise, and generational oppression be lifted off—and shut forever. You are strong and mighty in battle, and You war for me tonight. Let the gates of my mind lift to Your truth. Let the gates of my home lift to Your presence. Let my spiritual borders be guarded by fire, and let every passage that once gave the enemy legal ground be destroyed by Your Word.

I declare that You, O Lord, have entered in. The King of Glory reigns here. There is no room for evil. No room for fear. No room for invasion. The gates are lifted and You have come—and now, they are locked in place with Your glory inside. In Jesus' name, Amen.

SHIELD

SHIELDED BY EVERY WORD

> "Every word of God is flawless. He is a shield to those who take refuge in him.
> —Proverbs 30:5 WEB

Lord, every word that comes from Your mouth is flawless—a shield to those who take refuge in You. Tonight, I take refuge in Your Word. I rest beneath its promises. I take cover under its authority. When lies try to find me in the dark, I hold up the Word like a shield. When fear whispers, I raise the sword of truth. Let every flaming dart from the enemy dissolve before it reaches me.

Your Word defends me tonight—not just in theory, but in reality. Your promises are not distant—they are active and living around me. I declare that every verse You've spoken over my life stands as a barrier the enemy cannot penetrate. I do not just read the Word—I wear it like armor. It surrounds me. It guards me. It hides me in plain sight.

Let Your truth wrap around my mind, guarding me from anxiety. Let it blanket my body, shielding me from restlessness. Let Your Word be a wall of fire around my room and a fortress within my spirit. I declare that I am shielded by revelation, by truth, and by every flawless promise You have spoken. In Jesus' name, Amen.

Silence

He Sings While I Sleep

> Yahweh, your God, is among you, a mighty one who will save. He will rejoice over you with joy. He will calm you in his love. He will rejoice over you with singing.
> —Zephaniah 3:17 WEB

Mighty Warrior, the Lord who is near, I thank You that You rejoice over me with singing. In the quiet hours when darkness tries to speak, You raise Your voice in love and power. While the enemy plots, You sing. While fear whispers, You shout joy. Tonight, I silence every voice of torment and welcome the song of the Lord into my atmosphere.

I declare that Your voice is louder than the accuser. Your melodies drown out the murmurs of fear and anxiety. You rejoice over me—not reluctantly, but with delight. Let that sound fill every room. Let the song of the Lord replace every lie that has lingered. Let heavenly lyrics rewrite the narratives that try to haunt me in the dark.

Tonight, I receive Your love song. I let it saturate my mind. I silence the voice of condemnation and turn my ear to heaven. I will not meditate on fear—I will meditate on joy. I will not echo worry—I will echo worship. The Lord my God is in my midst, and He sings louder than the storm.

Let the silence be filled with Your sound.

In Jesus' name, Amen.

SHOW

LIGHT IN THE NIGHT SEASON

> He reveals the deep and secret things. He knows what is in the darkness, and the light dwells with him.
> —Daniel 2:22 WEB

Father, You are the God who reveals deep and hidden things. You know what is in the darkness, and light dwells with You. As I prepare to sleep tonight, I ask You to illuminate my spirit. Shine light on the things I cannot see. Unveil what is hidden. Reveal what has been confusing. Bring clarity to my waiting.

I do not fear the night, for in You there is no darkness at all. Let revelation come as I rest. Let insight awaken within me as I dream. Speak to me in visions. Guide me with divine impressions. Let mysteries become manageable. Let confusion give way to understanding. Show me what's ahead. Remind me of what's eternal.

You are not silent in the dark. You are not distant when I lie down. You walk with me into the shadows and bring brilliance where there was only uncertainty. Let every blind spot be revealed. Let every secret counsel of heaven be shared with me. I trust You to instruct me while I sleep and light my path for the days ahead.

Tonight, I sleep in the presence of the Revealer.

In Jesus' name, Amen.

Sleep

He Gives While I Rest

It is vain for you to rise up early, to stay up late, eating the bread of toil; for he gives sleep to his loved ones.
—Psalms 127:2 WEB

Tonight, I rest in divine rhythm. You give sleep to Your beloved, and not only sleep—but blessing in their sleep. I do not need to labor in the night. I do not need to strive in the shadows. You are the God who works while I rest. I lay down tonight, not in weakness, but in faith. You give, You restore, You build even while I dream.

Let this night be holy. Let this sleep be fruitful. I surrender to divine rest, and I receive divine provision. Fill my body with strength. Fill my spirit with fresh grace. Fill my mind with the peace that only You can give. Let everything I need for tomorrow begin to grow in the soil of tonight's surrender.

I reject the lie that nothing happens in rest. I believe the truth that You are active while I am still. I am not behind—I am beloved. I am not anxious—I am secure. I will not worry through the night. I will receive what You give while I sleep.

So I lie down in confidence. I rest in grace. And I will wake up with more than I had before I closed my eyes.

In Jesus' name, Amen.

DAY 5

SHUT

CHAINS BROKEN, GATES CLOSED

Now I will break his yoke from off you, and will burst your bonds apart."
—Nahum 1:13 WEB

Mighty Deliverer, tonight I declare the breaking of every yoke and the shattering of every chain. You have said that the enemy's grip will be torn from my neck, and I claim that promise now. Every bondage that has followed me into the night—mental torment, emotional heaviness, generational oppression—I now shut the door against it. I declare that the bars of captivity are broken, and the prison gates of fear and sin are closed forever.

Let every spiritual stronghold lose its strength tonight. I renounce all agreements with darkness, spoken or unspoken. I close every cycle of compromise, and I refuse to allow the enemy another night to manipulate, oppress, or distract me. My life is not available to evil. My sleep is not a playground for the demonic. The yoke has been destroyed by the anointing, and I stand free under the rule of Christ.

I now shut every gate behind me. The past will not pursue me. The bondage will not return. I am loosed from what once limited me, and I sleep tonight as a child of freedom, surrounded by victory.

In Jesus' name, Amen.

SHIELD

Faithful to Guard My Night

> But the Lord is faithful, who will establish you, and guard you from the evil one.
> —2 Thessalonians 3:3 WEB

Lord, I thank You that You are faithful. You have promised to strengthen and guard me from the evil one—and I believe it. While others may fear the unknown of nightfall, I rest in the certainty of Your presence. You are my shield—not temporary, not fragile, but eternal and unshakable. You cover me with strength, and You block every path the enemy would take to reach me.

Tonight, I surrender to the shelter of Your faithfulness. I declare that no evil can bypass the defense of my God. Every snare is exposed and broken. Every trap is overturned. Every curse is reversed. You are faithful not only to protect, but to keep me whole. You guard my soul from fear, my thoughts from despair, and my body from unrest.

Let angels be dispatched now to reinforce the shield around my home. Let every unseen attack be stopped by divine interception. Let every shadow be lit by Your glory. I lie down with full assurance that I am not alone—I am surrounded by the covenant-keeping God who neither forgets nor fails.

In Jesus' name, Amen.

SILENCE

NO WEAPON WILL SPEAK TONIGHT

> No weapon that is formed against you will prevail; and you will condemn every tongue that rises against you in judgment. This is the heritage of Yahweh's servants, and their righteousness is of me," says Yahweh.
> —Isaiah 54:17 WEB

Lord, tonight I take my place under the banner of Your authority, and I silence every weapon of the enemy. No lie, no accusation, no demonic whisper will prosper in my ears. Every tongue that rises against me is condemned—not because of my strength, but because of Your righteousness. I take authority over the night and command every dark voice to fall silent in the presence of truth.

I silence the inner critic that replays failure. I silence the voice of condemnation that disturbs my peace. I silence the enemy who reminds me of battles already won. You are my defender, and Your Word is my shield. Let no threat lodge in my heart. Let no fear sneak past my guard. Let no demonic word carry weight in my soul.

Let Your voice speak louder than every lie. Let Your truth echo in my dreams. Let Your presence be the final word in my mind tonight. I am not under assault—I am under covenant. And every weapon formed against me has already failed.

In Jesus' name, Amen.

Show

He Speaks While I Sleep

> For God speaks once, yes twice, though man pays no attention. In a dream, in a vision of the night, when deep sleep falls on men, in slumbering on the bed; Then he opens the ears of men, and seals their instruction,
> —Job 33:14-16 WEB

Father, tonight I tune my spirit to heaven's frequency. You do not wait for morning to speak—You visit me in dreams, You whisper in the silence, You counsel me as I sleep. You speak once, yes twice, in the stillness of night, and I declare that I will not miss Your voice. Let my heart remain sensitive. Let my mind be receptive. Let my spirit be alert even as my body rests.

Open the vaults of revelation and pour into me divine instruction. Warn me where danger hides. Show me where wisdom waits. Lead me into mysteries I cannot know by natural means. As I lay down, let visions come. As I rest, let dreams be birthed. I welcome Your holy interruption—wake me with purpose, stir me with clarity, whisper secrets that change my direction.

Let this night be a divine classroom, where Your Spirit teaches and trains me. May I rise not just rested, but instructed. May I carry the residue of revelation into my morning. I surrender this sleep to divine encounter. Speak, Lord—Your servant is listening.

In Jesus' name, Amen.

SLEEP

REST THAT REVIVES MY SPIRIT

> "Repent therefore, and turn again, that your sins may be blotted out, so that there may come times of refreshing from the presence of the Lord,
> —Acts 3:19 WEB

Lord, I come to this moment not merely seeking sleep, but rest that revives. You invite me to turn from weariness, to repent and return, so that times of refreshing may come from Your presence. I return to You tonight—not only from sin, but from self-reliance. I release the burdens I've carried. I lay down the striving. I open my soul to be refreshed.

Let this sleep be healing. Let it be holy. Let it be heavy with grace. Breathe on me tonight and wash away fatigue, sorrow, confusion, and stress. I receive the restoration that only comes from being in Your presence. Let my mind reset. Let my body recover. Let my spirit be revived by Your breath.

This is not just physical sleep—it is spiritual renewal. While I lie down, let revival begin within me. Prepare me in this rest for what You have waiting when I rise. I trust You to do in eight hours what I could not achieve in eight days—complete rest, total reset, supernatural restoration.

I receive refreshing now, and I sleep in peace.

In Jesus' name, Amen.

DAY 6

SHUT

THE DESTROYER MUST PASS OVER

> For Yahweh will pass through to strike the Egyptians; and when he sees the blood on the lintel, and on the two door posts, Yahweh will pass over the door, and will not allow the destroyer to come in to your houses to strike you.
> —Exodus 12:23 WEB

Tonight, I stand under the blood covering of the Lamb, and I declare with boldness: the destroyer must pass over me. Just as You protected Israel in the night of judgment, so now I claim the same covenant protection over my life. I apply the blood of Jesus to the doorposts of my mind, my home, my family, and everything under my care. I shut the gate to death, calamity, and disaster—none shall enter in.

Let the destroyer see the mark and turn away. Let judgment pass, let darkness pass, let every demonic assignment be halted at the threshold. No spirit of fear, no power of torment, no messenger of destruction has legal access to my night. I declare my atmosphere sealed, my home secured, and my life hidden in Christ.

You are the God who watches over Your own. As I sleep tonight, I trust that heaven's eye remains vigilant on my behalf. I will not fear what walks in the shadows, for the blood speaks louder than any curse. The enemy must pass over. My house is off-limits to harm. The gate is shut and guarded by glory. In Jesus' name, Amen.

SHIELD

MY ROCK AND FORTRESS

> Yahweh is my rock, my fortress, and my deliverer; my God, my rock, in whom I take refuge; my shield, and the horn of my salvation, my high tower.
> —Psalms 18:2 WEB

Lord, tonight I take refuge in You—my rock, my fortress, my deliverer. You are my shield, the horn of my salvation, and my stronghold. I do not stand in my own strength tonight—I hide myself in You. When the winds of fear blow, I remain unmoved. When the arrows of the enemy fly, I remain untouched. For You are my refuge, and in You I am completely covered.

Wrap me in the strength of Your name. Cover me with the power of Your righteousness. Let the shield of faith absorb every lie, every dart, every accusation that tries to take root in my mind. Surround me with songs of deliverance. Set angels at every corner of my home. I declare that nothing sent to harm me will succeed, because I am not exposed—I am encased in Your strength.

I rest tonight under divine security. Let every unseen danger crash against the walls of Your protection. Let my mind rest in the truth that I am not alone. My God is my shield, and nothing formed against me will prevail. I am hidden in the safety of the Rock who never fails.

In Jesus' name, Amen.

Silence

Hidden from the Strife of Tongues

> Oh how great is your goodness, which you have laid up for those who fear you, which you have worked for those who take refuge in you, before the sons of men! In the shelter of your presence you will hide them from the plotting of man. You will keep them secretly in a dwelling away from the strife of tongues.
> —Psalms 31:19-20 WEB

Father, You are my secret place, and tonight I hide in the shelter of Your presence. You store up goodness for those who fear You and hide them from the plots and slanders of men. So now I take refuge beneath Your covering, and I silence every lying tongue and whispering spirit that seeks to disturb my peace.

Let every voice of accusation fall silent. Let every mocking thought be muzzled. Let every demonic whisper that would speak in the night be drowned out by the sound of Your nearness. I take refuge in the sanctuary of Your love, and in that place, no enemy can reach me. You surround me with favor like a shield and cover me in Your tabernacle, far from the strife of tongues.

Even now, I feel Your nearness. Even now, the chaos quiets. The voice of the accuser cannot find me here. The noise of fear cannot enter. I am hidden—not only from men, but from every spiritual force that would torment me. I will sleep in silence, not because the war has ceased, but because the Lord of Hosts has silenced the battlefield.

In Jesus' name, Amen.

Show

Secrets Shared in Stillness

> The friendship of Yahweh is with those who fear him. He will show them his covenant.
> —Psalms 25:14 WEB

Lord, I thank You that You confide in those who fear You. You don't shout over the noise—you whisper in the stillness. So tonight, I quiet my heart and position my spirit to receive what only You can reveal. I long not only for protection in the night, but revelation. Speak to me as one You trust. Show me what is hidden. Reveal Your heart in the darkness.

As I sleep, open up the scrolls of heaven. Make known to me Your plans. Teach me Your ways. Let wisdom rise in my dreams and direction emerge from my rest. I am not asking for empty dreams—I'm asking for divine communication. I am Your servant, and I am listening. Visit me, speak to me, and guide me.

You promised to share secrets with those who revere You—and I am here, expectant, yielded, and alert. Even in sleep, I remain Yours. Illuminate what I've missed. Show me the path ahead. Let the night hours become a wellspring of wisdom.

In Jesus' name, Amen.

Sleep

Rest in the Land of Promise

> "Remember the word which Moses the servant of Yahweh commanded you, saying, 'Yahweh your God gives you rest, and will give you this land.
> —Joshua 1:13 WEB

Father, tonight I rest in the promise that You have given me the land, and You have given me rest. This is not just physical rest—it is covenant rest. The kind of rest that comes when the battle has already been won, when the promise has already been given, and when the presence of the Lord surrounds me like a river of peace.

I lay down knowing that I am in the territory of grace. I am not striving for victory—I am sleeping in it. You have commanded me to remember that You are the One who gives rest, and I receive it now. I release every tension, every striving, every weight. I will not carry what You already took to the cross.

Let this be a night of real rest—where my body is restored, my soul is renewed, and my mind is washed clean. Let me sleep as one who is secure in the promise, anchored in the Word, and confident in the goodness of God. I wake tomorrow in strength because I lay down tonight in trust.

In Jesus' name, Amen.

DAY 7

SHUT

A WALL OF FIRE AROUND ME

> For I,' says Yahweh, 'will be to her a wall of fire around it, and I will be the glory in the middle of her.
> —Zechariah 2:5 WEB

Lord of Hosts, tonight I declare the fire of Your presence surrounds me. You have promised to be a wall of fire around Your people and the glory within. I claim that covenant now over my home, my room, my body, my spirit—every place where I dwell, let it burn with divine fire. I shut the gate to every spiritual intruder and decree: no weapon, no curse, no wandering spirit can penetrate the perimeter of Your protection.

Let the fire of the Lord consume every demonic assignment sent against me in the night. Let it expose every dark plan and reduce it to ash. I declare my home is off-limits to evil. My dreams are not accessible to torment. The fire of Your presence is my fortress, and nothing unclean can cross its boundary.

Where fear once crept in, let flames now blaze. Where spiritual weakness once lingered, let supernatural fire arise. I am sealed, I am guarded, I am hidden in the brilliance of Your burning presence. Let this wall of fire stand through the night and into the dawn. I sleep behind a flame the enemy cannot cross. In Jesus' name, Amen.

SHIELD

My Strength, My Shield, My Song

> Yahweh is my strength and my shield. My heart has trusted in him, and I am helped. Therefore my heart greatly rejoices. With my song I will thank him.
> —Psalms 28:7 WEB

Father, tonight I rejoice in Your faithful protection. You are my strength and my shield—my heart trusts in You, and I am helped. You are not a distant defender; You are near, surrounding me with songs of deliverance and upholding me with unseen power. I rest tonight in the arms of the One who never fails.

When darkness tries to approach, You stand in the way. When fear knocks on the door, You answer with strength. I declare that every fiery dart, every whispered lie, every form of harm is intercepted by Your mighty shield. You defend me without fail. You cover me without ceasing. I do not sleep in my own power—I sleep in Your supernatural care.

Let Your shield rise between me and every fear. Between me and every night terror. Between me and every accusation from the pit of hell. My body is at ease, my mind is protected, and my heart is secure. I trust You, Lord, and You help me. I sing for joy even as I lie down, for the One who keeps me never slumbers.

In Jesus' name, Amen.

SILENCE

I Will Wait in Praise

> I will give you thanks forever, because you have done it. I will hope in your name, for it is good, in the presence of your saints.
> —Psalms 52:9 WEB

Lord, tonight I silence the voices of disappointment, fear, and impatience. I choose to lift up praise, even before the answer comes. You are good, and I will wait on You with confidence. I silence the voice that tells me You are late, the whisper that says You've forgotten me, the lie that tempts me to doubt Your goodness. I lift up Your name instead, for You have done great things.

Let every tormenting voice fall silent in the light of my gratitude. I praise You not because everything is perfect, but because You are worthy. My waiting will not become worrying. My silence will not be filled with fear—it will be filled with worship. I rest tonight, trusting that You are working even now.

You have been faithful before, and You will be faithful again. I silence my striving. I release control. And I declare: I will praise You forever for what You have already done, and what You're doing even now behind the veil of night. My heart is steady, my spirit is calm. I wait in peace, and I worship in silence.

In Jesus' name, Amen.

Show

In All My Ways, Guide Me

> In all your ways acknowledge him, and he will make your paths straight.
> —Proverbs 3:6 WEB

Lord, I surrender every path to You tonight. Your Word says that if I acknowledge You in all my ways, You will direct my paths. So now, I open up every uncertain road, every crossroad in my life, and I invite You to lead me—even while I sleep. Speak to me in the night watches. Guide me in dreams. Align my decisions with heaven's agenda.

I don't just need rest—I need revelation. I don't just want sleep—I want strategy. Let the way ahead become clear. Show me the steps I've missed. Illuminate what's hidden. Give me peace about what You've confirmed and unrest about what You've not ordained. I yield every plan to You now.

Tonight, I make room for Your voice. In visions or whispers, in peace or warning, speak. Guide me with Your eye. I trust that when I wake, I will rise with new direction, renewed clarity, and strengthened obedience. You never lead astray. You always make straight paths.

In Jesus' name, Amen.

Sleep

You Satisfy My Soul with Rest

> For I have satiated the weary soul, and I have replenished every sorrowful soul."
> —Jeremiah 31:25 WEB

Lord, I come to You tonight, weary yet willing, empty yet expectant. Your promise declares that You satisfy the weary soul and refresh the faint. I receive that now. I don't just need sleep—I need soul rest. Let the deep places in me be refreshed. Let my spirit drink deeply from Your presence and my mind be reset by Your peace.

You know the battles I've faced. You know the things I haven't spoken out loud. You know what has drained me. So now, I lay it all before You. I let go of the heaviness and take hold of Your rest. Breathe over me tonight, Holy Spirit. Calm every racing thought. Soothe every aching place. Fill every dry well.

I declare that this sleep will not be interrupted, invaded, or stolen. It will be holy. It will be healing. It will be filled with Your presence. I do not fear the dark, because the Light is within me. I do not fear tomorrow, because You are already there. Let this night be a well of satisfaction. I will lie down and be restored.

In Jesus' name, Amen.

DAY 8

SHUT

THE DEVOURER IS REBUKED

> I will rebuke the devourer for your sakes, and he shall not destroy the fruits of your ground; neither shall your vine cast its fruit before its time in the field," says Yahweh of Armies.
> —Malachi 3:11 WEB

Faithful Father, tonight I take my stand in the authority of Your Word. You have promised to rebuke the devourer for my sake, and so I shut the gates of my life to every consuming force. I declare that no thief, no destroyer, no spiritual predator has access to what You have blessed. Every portal through which lack, delay, confusion, or destruction once entered—I now seal by the blood of Jesus.

Let the devourer be silenced at my borders. Let the locust be driven from my field. Let what I've sown in faith remain untouched by the hands of darkness. I declare that my home is not vulnerable. My mind is not open to torment. My dreams are not exposed to theft. Heaven has drawn a line, and the devourer cannot cross it.

I rest tonight knowing that my fruit will not be stolen, my efforts will not be wasted, and my peace will not be eaten away. I sleep in security because the Lord has rebuked every spiritual devourer on my behalf. My household is guarded. My legacy is protected. My gates are shut to the enemy. In Jesus' name, Amen.

SHIELD

HELP FROM HIS HOLY HEAVEN

> Now I know that Yahweh saves his anointed. He will answer him from his holy heaven, with the saving strength of his right hand.
> —Psalms 20:6 WEB

Lord, tonight I rejoice in the truth that You save Your anointed and answer from Your holy heaven. I am not uncovered, not alone, not defenseless—I am backed by the power of the Almighty. While others trust in their strength, I trust in the name of the Lord. You are my shield, and I stand beneath Your divine help and intervention.

Let heaven's power surround my sleep. Let angelic reinforcements defend my borders. Let every plan of darkness fall flat before it finds me. I declare that my name is known in heaven, and that heaven's shield surrounds me now. I do not need to be afraid of the terrors of night or the arrows that fly in silence—Your help is near, and Your glory goes before me.

I rest tonight not in the hope of protection, but in the certainty of it. My room is filled with the covering of Your presence. My spirit is clothed in salvation. My mind is guarded by the shield of Your favor. I lie down in safety, wrapped in answered prayer.

In Jesus' name, Amen.

SILENCE

FEAR HAS NO VOICE HERE

> Don't you be afraid, for I am with you. Don't be dismayed, for I am your God. I will strengthen you. Yes, I will help you. Yes, I will uphold you with the right hand of my righteousness.
> —Isaiah 41:10 WEB

Father, I declare tonight: I will not fear. You are with me. I will not be dismayed, for You are my God. You strengthen me, help me, and uphold me with Your righteous right hand. Every voice that stirs panic, anxiety, or despair—I silence you now in Jesus' name. You have no authority in my thoughts. You have no claim on my rest.

Let every whisper of dread be drowned in the assurance of God's presence. Let the tormenting lies of insufficiency and doom fall silent. My ears are tuned to the voice of truth. My heart is steady in the knowledge of Your nearness. Fear will not dictate my night. Doubt will not narrate my dreams.

I proclaim peace over my atmosphere and declare that all spiritual noise must cease. Let the hush of heaven settle over me now. Let the quiet confidence of Your Word fill every corner of my heart. You are not only with me, You are fighting for me—and in that, I rest.

In Jesus' name, Amen.

Show

The Kingdom Is Mine to Receive

> Don't be afraid, little flock, for it is your Father's good pleasure to give you the Kingdom.
> —Luke 12:32 WEB

Gracious Father, I thank You for the unshakable truth that it is Your good pleasure to give me the Kingdom. I receive that assurance tonight—not just in principle, but in revelation. Show me the beauty of Your reign in the stillness of this night. As I sleep, let Your Spirit open the windows of heaven and reveal to me more of Your heart, more of Your purpose, more of my inheritance in You.

Let dreams be filled with glimpses of glory. Let my heart be flooded with vision. I don't just want rest—I want encounter. I don't just want quiet—I want revelation. Let divine mysteries unfold while I sleep. Let direction come without striving. Let joy rise from heavenly perspective.

Father, speak to me in the quiet moments and whisper truth in the deep chambers of my soul. I open myself to receive kingdom insight, eternal priorities, and divine wisdom. Lead me into a deeper understanding of Your will and delight.

In Jesus' name, Amen.

SLEEP

COME TO ME AND REST

> "Come to me, all you who labor and are heavily burdened, and I will give you rest. Take my yoke upon you, and learn from me, for I am gentle and humble in heart; and you will find rest for your souls.
> —Matthew 11:28-29 WEB

Jesus, tonight I respond to Your call: "Come to Me, all who are weary." I come—tired in body, weary in soul, stretched in mind—and I lay everything at Your feet. I take Your yoke upon me now, and I exchange my burdens for Your rest. This is not a shallow pause, but a deep and holy rest that renews the spirit and anchors the soul.

Let my bed be an altar tonight, where surrender meets peace. I choose to let go. I choose to breathe deeply of grace. I will not carry tomorrow into tonight. I will not relive what cannot be changed. You are gentle and lowly in heart, and I receive Your rest as a sacred gift.

Let every muscle release its tension. Let every anxious thought be hushed. Let every weary corner of my being drink deeply from the fountain of Your presence. I will lie down and sleep—not as a slave of time or task, but as a beloved child who trusts her Father's care.

I rest because You have invited me to. I sleep because You have made it safe to do so.

In Jesus' name, Amen.

DAY 9

SHUT

SURROUNDED LIKE MOUNT ZION

> As the mountains surround Jerusalem, so Yahweh surrounds his people from this time forward and forever more.
> —Psalms 125:2 WEB

Lord, tonight I declare that as the mountains surround Jerusalem, so You surround me—now and forever. I am not exposed to the enemy's reach, not vulnerable to unseen forces. You encircle me with Your power, and I shut the gates to every spiritual intrusion that seeks to steal, distract, or destroy in the night. No darkness may cross the boundary You've established.

Let every backdoor to fear be sealed. Let every hidden entry point used by torment or temptation be closed and guarded by angelic hosts. My life is encamped by glory, and no weapon can slip through. I am not only covered—I am surrounded. You are my rear guard. You go before me. You are on every side, and I rest in this divine perimeter.

Tonight, I am not anxious about what surrounds me because I am surrounded by You. I dwell in safety, and I will not be shaken. The gates are shut. The shield is up. The blood has been applied. I sleep inside the circle of Your covenant presence.

In Jesus' name, Amen.

SHIELD

NOTHING WITHHELD FROM THE UPRIGHT

> For Yahweh God is a sun and a shield. Yahweh will give grace and glory. He withholds no good thing from those who walk blamelessly.
> —Psalms 84:11 WEB

Father, You are a sun and a shield. You give grace and glory, and You withhold no good thing from those who walk uprightly. I receive that promise over my life tonight. I declare that I am not under lack, not uncovered, not forsaken. You are both my provider and my protector, lighting my path and guarding my steps, even as I sleep.

Let Your shield of favor surround me. Let Your hand deflect every arrow meant to harm me. I rest beneath the canopy of Your covenant, and I boldly say: no lack shall overtake me, no shadow shall intimidate me, no fear shall find me. You are a shield about me and the glory that lifts my head.

I am not trying to earn protection—I walk in it by faith. You are my shield and exceedingly great reward. Let goodness chase me. Let mercy encircle me. Let Your faithfulness guard every side. While others wonder if You will show up, I lie down knowing You already have.

In Jesus' name, Amen.

SILENCE

HIDDEN IN HIS PAVILION

> For in the day of trouble, he will keep me secretly in his pavilion. In the secret place of his tabernacle, he will hide me. He will lift me up on a rock.
> —Psalms 27:5 WEB

Father, You are my safe place. When trouble rises, You hide me in Your pavilion; You set me high upon a rock. So tonight, I silence every voice that says I'm exposed or abandoned. I am not left to defend myself in the dark. I am hidden in You, tucked under the wings of divine safety where no lie can reach me and no fear can rule.

I shut down the internal noise of doubt, the external noise of culture, and the spiritual noise of accusation. Let only Your whisper be heard tonight. Drown out the sound of shame. Cancel the soundtrack of condemnation. Let this night be wrapped in quiet confidence—because I am hidden in the One who is greater than all.

Tonight, the darkness may speak, but I won't listen. I'll stay in the secret place of Your presence until every storm passes. I won't respond to fear—I will rest in faith. I declare silence over every voice not sent by You.

In Jesus' name, Amen.

SHOW

REVELATION IN THE NIGHT

> that the God of our Lord Jesus Christ, the Father of glory, may give to you a spirit of wisdom and revelation in the knowledge of him; having the eyes of your hearts enlightened, that you may know what is the hope of his calling, and what are the riches of the glory of his inheritance in the saints,
> —Ephesians 1:17-18 WEB

Father of glory, tonight I ask You to give me the Spirit of wisdom and revelation in the knowledge of You. As I rest, open the eyes of my heart to see what cannot be seen with natural sight. I desire more than dreams—I desire divine insight. I ask not just for sleep, but for spiritual enlightenment. Show me what You are doing in this season of my life.

Unveil Your strategies. Whisper Your heart. Reveal purpose and identity with clarity that outlasts the night. Let the eyes of my understanding be flooded with light, even in the quietness of this room. While the world sleeps blindly, I ask You to awaken my spirit to heavenly activity.

Give me divine downloads while I rest. Let mysteries become manageable. Let scripture take root in deeper ways. I yield to You tonight, Holy Spirit—teach me, lead me, reveal to me what aligns with heaven. I expect encounter. I prepare for vision. Speak, Lord—Your servant is listening.

In Jesus' name, Amen.

SLEEP

SOARING IN MY STILLNESS

> But those who wait for Yahweh will renew their strength. They will mount up with wings like eagles. They will run, and not be weary. They will walk, and not faint.
> —Isaiah 40:31 WEB

Everlasting God, tonight I receive Your promise: that those who wait on You will renew their strength. I come not with striving, but with stillness. I wait on You not with fear, but with faith. And as I lie down to sleep, I trust that You will restore, renew, and elevate me—even in rest.

Let this night be more than recovery—let it be renewal. Cause my strength to rise as I cease from my own efforts. Cause my spirit to soar even while my eyes close. I will not grow weary in the waiting. I will not faint in the process. You are my strength, and You are restoring me from the inside out.

I trust You with the work I cannot do while I sleep. I release the burdens I've carried. I cast all my cares upon You. And I lie down knowing that rest is not weakness—it is worship. I will rise with new strength, new vision, and new joy because I chose to rest in the shadow of the Almighty.

In Jesus' name, Amen.

DAY 10

SHUT

YOU DREW NEAR AND DEFENDED ME

> You came near in the day that I called on you. You said, "Don't be afraid." Lord, you have pleaded the causes of my soul. You have redeemed my life.
> —Lamentations 3:57-58 WEB

Lord, tonight I remember how You drew near when I called on You. You did not delay. You whispered, "Do not fear," and You took up my case. You are my Redeemer, and I declare now that every open door of fear, accusation, or torment is shut by the authority of Your defense. I am not vulnerable to the attacks of the night—I am under divine protection.

Every voice that has come to accuse me, every spirit that has come to disturb my rest, every gate the enemy has tried to sneak through—I seal it shut in the name of Jesus. Let the courtroom of heaven speak for me. You have pleaded my cause and rescued my soul from destruction. I need not defend myself, for the Judge has already ruled in my favor.

Let every threat be silenced. Let every plan to bring confusion be overturned. I shut the door on shame, rejection, and regret. I lie down tonight with no fear of condemnation because You, O Lord, have defended me. In Jesus' name, Amen.

SHIELD

You Lifted Me Up

A Psalm. A Song for the Dedication of the Temple. By David. I will extol you, Yahweh, for you have raised me up, and have not made my foes to rejoice over me.
—Psalms 30:1 WEB

Father, I praise You tonight for being the One who lifted me out of the pit. When the enemy thought he had me, You raised me up. You did not let my foes rejoice over me, and You will not let them triumph tonight. I am shielded not by human strength but by Your mercy and grace. You are my covering, my stronghold, and my high place.

Let Your shield rise around me now. I take refuge in the shadow of Your wings. Let no lingering guilt, fear, or spiritual assault touch me. I declare that I am untouchable under Your defense. What tried to pull me down cannot reach me now. You have exalted me above the reach of torment.

As I lay down, I do not fear the night. You surround me with songs of deliverance. You lift me above my enemies and preserve my soul with unfailing love. I rest tonight in the safety of Your hands, shielded by Your victory.

In Jesus' name, Amen.

Silence

The God of Peace Will Crush

> And the God of peace will quickly crush Satan under your feet. The grace of our Lord Jesus Christ be with you.
> —Romans 16:20 WEB

Lord of Peace, tonight I declare that every voice of the adversary is crushed beneath Your feet. You are not only my Savior—you are the God of war, and You promised to crush Satan under my feet shortly. So I silence the hiss of accusation, the whisper of intimidation, and the growl of discouragement. The enemy is defeated, and his voice is stripped of power.

Let the roar of heaven thunder louder than the lies of hell. Let every anxious thought be cast down. Let the noise of warfare give way to the peace of victory. I refuse to lie awake rehearsing battles already won. I silence the voice of yesterday's failures and tomorrow's fears. The final word belongs to You.

Tonight, the enemy is beneath my feet. His strategies are exposed. His curses are cancelled. His voice is void. I lie down in the stillness of victory, declaring that peace reigns in this house and in my soul.

In Jesus' name, Amen.

Show

Open My Eyes to Wonder

> Open my eyes, that I may see wondrous things out of your law.
> —Psalms 119:18 WEB

Father, as I sleep, I ask You to open my eyes—not just physically, but spiritually. Uncover what I've overlooked. Reveal truth buried beneath distractions. Let Your Word come alive within me even in the quiet of the night. I hunger for vision that only You can give. Show me the hidden wonders of Your law, the deep truths of Your purpose, and the things I've missed in the rush of the day.

Give me a heart that sees beyond the surface. Unlock insight through dreams. Let instruction flow like a river in the stillness. Shine light on the path ahead. Reveal the next step, the buried promise, the forgotten word. I want to see as You see.

Let my rest be pregnant with revelation. Speak, Lord—Your servant is ready to perceive. Awaken the prophetic within me. Enlighten the eyes of my heart, that I may walk in greater understanding of who You are and what You're doing in this season of my life.

In Jesus' name, Amen.

SLEEP

HE LEADS ME BESIDE STILL WATERS

> He makes me lie down in green pastures. He leads me beside still waters.
> —Psalms 23:2 WEB

Good Shepherd, tonight I surrender to the still waters You've prepared for me. I release the chaos of the day. I yield every burden of my soul. You lead me, gently and faithfully, into rest that restores. I will not resist the peace You've promised. I will not wrestle with the night. I lie down because You've made it safe to do so.

Restore my soul, Lord. Bring back what was drained. Rebuild what was broken. Refresh what has been weary. You are not just my protector—You are my peace. I lay down on the pastures of Your promise, and I drink deeply from the stillness You provide. Every part of me aligns with Your rhythm tonight.

Let my dreams reflect Your goodness. Let my breathing slow under the weight of Your love. Let me wake up whole. I trust You with my mind, my body, and my future. You are with me in the day, and You are nearer still in the night.

Tonight, I sleep beside still waters and rise with a soul restored.

In Jesus' name, Amen.

DAY 11

SHUT

WHEN THE ENEMY RUSHES IN

> So shall they fear Yahweh's name from the west, and his glory from the rising of the sun; for he will come as a rushing stream, which Yahweh's breath drives.
> —Isaiah 59:19 WEB

Lord, tonight I declare with boldness: when the enemy comes in like a flood, the Spirit of the Lord will lift up a standard against him. I will not be swept away by fear, by lies, or by attacks sent to overwhelm me. You are the One who raises the banner of victory and shuts the gates against the tide of darkness.

I shut the door to panic, to spiritual ambush, and to every storm engineered to steal my rest. I declare that the floodwaters will not rise over my head, because You've drawn a line the enemy cannot cross. The gates of my mind are sealed in peace. The entry points of my heart are guarded by truth. The Spirit of the Lord is my defense.

Let every surge of darkness be repelled by divine resistance. Let every late-night anxiety, every hidden attack, every whispering fear be silenced by the roar of Your standard. I dwell tonight beneath the covering of the Most High. The flood may rise, but it will not enter.

In Jesus' name, Amen.

SHIELD

COVERED IN BATTLE AND STILL

> Yahweh, the Lord, the strength of my salvation, you have covered my head in the day of battle.
> —Psalms 140:7 WEB

Mighty God, You are my saving strength in the day of battle. When the warfare rises, You are not caught off guard. You surround me with deliverance, and You train my hands to war—even in the unseen realm of the night. I am not defenseless in the dark. I am covered, armed, and protected by Your mighty hand.

Let every arrow fired in secret be intercepted by Your shield. Let every scheme that rises against me be overturned before it reaches its mark. You know how to defend me in ways I cannot see. While I sleep, You surround me with strength. You block the path of destruction and stand between me and danger.

Tonight, I do not fear surprise attacks or sudden blows. You are the One who covers my head in the day of battle, and You are covering me now in the stillness of night. My shield is up. My soul is guarded. My rest is secure.

In Jesus' name, Amen.

Silence

Peace Be Still

> He makes the storm a calm, so that its waves are still.
> —Psalms 107:29 WEB

Prince of Peace, I invite You into every storm—spoken or unspoken, seen or invisible. Just as You stood in the boat and commanded the winds and waves, I ask You now to speak to every chaos in my life: "Peace, be still." I silence every wave of fear, every wind of anxiety, every crashing thought that seeks to wreck my stillness.

Let the voice of the accuser be hushed. Let the noise of the world fade into nothing. Let every spiritual storm sent to disturb my rest be brought under Your command. You are not intimidated by the wind, nor moved by the waves. You are in the boat with me, and that alone is enough.

Tonight, I will not let fear speak louder than faith. I will not allow restlessness to rule over peace. You have authority over the night, and You are present here. Speak, Lord, and calm the storm within me.

In Jesus' name, Amen.

SHOW

WISDOM IN THE NIGHT WATCHES

> But if any of you lacks wisdom, let him ask of God, who gives to all liberally and without reproach; and it will be given to him.
> —James 1:5 WEB

Holy Spirit, Giver of wisdom, I ask tonight for insight that only You can provide. You give generously to all who ask without reproach, and I ask in faith, without doubting. Let this be a night not only of rest, but of revelation. As I sleep, unlock the answers I've been seeking. Speak through dreams, confirm through peace, and guide through stillness.

Illuminate what's been confusing. Clarify what's been cloudy. Give me wisdom for what's coming, discernment for what's hidden, and understanding beyond my years. I open my spirit to receive heavenly counsel. I will not lean on my own understanding—I look to You, my Teacher and Guide.

Tonight, make the complex simple. Turn the fog of decision-making into crystal clarity. Let wisdom rise in me like dawn, and let me wake with answers I didn't have when I lay down. Speak, Lord—my heart is listening even while I rest.

In Jesus' name, Amen.

SLEEP

ENTER THE SABBATH OF HIS REST

> There remains therefore a Sabbath rest for the people of God.
> —Hebrews 4:9 WEB

Father, I step tonight into the rest You've already prepared for me. There remains a Sabbath rest for the people of God, and I enter that rest by faith. I cease from my own striving and release every burden I've carried today. I do not have to earn rest—I receive it. I don't have to fight for peace—it's already mine in Christ.

Let this be holy sleep—rest that restores every fiber of my being. Let every muscle relax. Let my breath align with heaven's rhythm. Let my mind calm under the assurance that You are at work even when I am not. I don't just want to sleep—I want to be renewed, recalibrated, and restored.

I yield to the rhythm of grace. I say no to anxiety. I surrender to divine stillness. I enter this rest not as an escape, but as a sacred trust. You are the Lord of the Sabbath, and You give sleep to Your beloved.

So I receive this night as a gift, and I enter into rest.

In Jesus' name, Amen.

DAY 12

SHUT

HIDE ME IN THE SHADOW

> Keep me as the apple of your eye. Hide me under the shadow of your wings, from the wicked who oppress me, my deadly enemies, who surround me.
> —Psalms 17:8-9 WEB

Father, I come under Your covering tonight and declare that I am hidden in the shadow of Your wings. I shut every gateway of vulnerability, every entry point of fear, and every portal that spiritual enemies could use to approach me in the night. You said You would keep me as the apple of Your eye—and I believe You.

Hide me from those who rise up against me in the spirit. Hide me from ambushes I cannot see, traps I do not know about, and attacks that are waiting to unfold in the shadows. I shut the door to every lurking enemy. I seal every spiritual border around my life with the blood of Jesus.

Let the eyes of my enemies go blind in the night. Let their hands be weakened, their weapons shattered, their curses nullified. I am not exposed—I am enveloped by the glory of God. You are my refuge, and I trust in You. The night may come, but it will not overcome.

In Jesus' name, Amen.

SHIELD

My Fortress, My Deliverer

> *By David.* Blessed be Yahweh, my rock, who teaches my hands to war, and my fingers to battle: my loving kindness, my fortress, my high tower, my deliverer, my shield, and he in whom I take refuge; who subdues my people under me.
> —Psalms 144:1-2 WEB

O Lord, my Rock and my Redeemer, You are my steadfast love and my fortress. You are my high tower and shield, the One in whom I take refuge. As I enter this night, I do so surrounded by Your strength. I declare that every direction I face is covered by Your covenant. My life is not unguarded—my God Himself is my defense.

I do not place my confidence in locks or alarms, but in You. You train my hands for war and my fingers for battle—even in the spirit. I take up Your truth, Your righteousness, and Your peace as my armor. You are the One who subdues enemies under my feet and keeps me standing when I should have fallen.

As I lie down tonight, I do so under divine military protection. Let angels stand guard. Let the blood of Jesus mark the borders. Let Your shield wrap around me as fire and glory. I fear no ambush, no arrow, no snare—for my Deliverer is near.

In Jesus' name, Amen.

Silence

Tread on Serpents in Peace

> Behold, I give you authority to tread on serpents and scorpions, and over all the power of the enemy. Nothing will in any way hurt you.
> —Luke 10:19 WEB

Lord Jesus, tonight I rest in the authority You have given me. You said, "Behold, I have given you authority to tread on serpents and scorpions, and over all the power of the enemy, and nothing shall by any means harm you." I take hold of that truth and silence every hissing lie that says otherwise.

I quiet the voices of intimidation, manipulation, and fear. I trample on every whisper of condemnation. The serpent's tongue has no right to speak to me. The accuser has no place in my atmosphere. I command every unclean spirit to be silent and retreat. My peace is not up for negotiation.

Let Your voice be the only sound in this night. Let the peace of Christ rule in my heart and drive out confusion, chatter, and torment. I speak stillness to my mind and quiet to my spirit. I rest tonight with confidence—nothing shall by any means harm me.

In Jesus' name, Amen.

Show

Led by the Eye of God

> I will instruct you and teach you in the way which you shall go. I will counsel you with my eye on you.
> —Psalms 32:8 WEB

Wise and gracious Father, I thank You that You will instruct me and teach me in the way I should go. You will guide me with Your eye. So now, in the stillness of this night, I ask You to reveal direction I cannot find on my own. I open the eyes of my heart to see what You are showing, to sense what You are speaking, and to align with what You are planning.

Lead me through dreams if You choose. Guide me through the peace of Your presence. Reveal what I need for tomorrow, and prepare me while I rest. I don't seek answers in my own strength—I wait for Your direction. Show me the path. Show me the pitfalls. Show me the promise. I will not walk blindly when I have access to Your wisdom.

As I sleep, let there be supernatural downloads. Let confusion unravel. Let clarity come. I trust that when I rise, I will rise with instruction from heaven.

In Jesus' name, Amen.

SLEEP

LIFE, PEACE, AND HOLY REST

> The fear of Yahweh leads to life, then contentment; he rests
> and will not be touched by trouble.
> —Proverbs 19:23 WEB

Lord, Your Word declares that the fear of the Lord leads to life, and whoever has it rests satisfied, untouched by harm. I receive that word tonight as a covering over my sleep. I do not lie down in dread, but in holy expectation. This will be a night of life-filled rest, where my soul is renewed, my body restored, and my mind refreshed.

I lay aside every anxious thought. I turn off every mental noise. I yield to the peace that passes all understanding. Let this be more than sleep—let it be sacred stillness, where Your Spirit breathes over every weary part of me.

You have said I will be untouched by harm, and I believe You. So I lie down in trust, not tension; in praise, not panic. I receive the life-giving rest that comes only from the presence of God. Let this be holy sleep, steeped in Your peace and secured in Your love.

In Jesus' name, Amen.

DAY 13

SHUT

PRESERVED FROM ALL EVIL

> Yahweh will keep you from all evil. He will keep your soul. Yahweh will keep your going out and your coming in, from this time forward, and forever more.
> —Psalms 121:7-8 WEB

Faithful God, tonight I declare that You are preserving me from all evil—every form, every face, every plan. You are watching over my life. I shut every gate that might allow harm to enter. I seal off every spiritual breach and declare that my coming in and going out, this night and forevermore, is secured by Your Word.

I cancel every midnight assignment of destruction, every nocturnal affliction, every spirit of harassment and fear. No evil shall enter my dwelling. No unclean thing shall approach my soul. The blood of Jesus surrounds me like a wall of fire, and the name of the Lord is a strong tower around me.

I thank You, Lord, that while I sleep, You keep watch. My doors are locked in the natural, but more importantly, they are sealed in the spirit. I will not be touched, disturbed, or infiltrated. You are the Keeper of my life.

In Jesus' name, Amen.

SHIELD

Flawless Shield of My God

As for God, his way is perfect. Yahweh's word is tested. He is a shield to all those who take refuge in him.
—2 Samuel 22:31 WEB

O Lord, Your way is perfect. Your Word is proven. You are a shield to all who trust in You. Tonight, I place my full trust in the integrity of who You are. You are not just a protector—you are my personal Defender, my flawless Shield, and the One who encircles me in divine security.

Let no flaw be found in my covering tonight. Let no hole exist in my hedge. I rest under the shield that never fails, the covering that never cracks, the protection that never sleeps. Arrows may fly by night, but they will fall short. Threats may form, but they will never prosper.

You are my hiding place, my deliverer, my defense. The battlefield of the mind is quieted because I know who surrounds me. Let Your shield repel every demonic dart, absorb every fiery accusation, and deflect every blow aimed at my soul.

In Jesus' name, Amen.

Silence

Though I Fall, I Rise

> Don't rejoice against me, my enemy. When I fall, I will arise. When I sit in darkness, Yahweh will be a light to me.
> —Micah 7:8 WEB

Father, even if I stumble, I will rise. Even if darkness surrounds me, it will not overtake me. I silence every voice tonight that says my fall is final. I shut down the accusations that tell me I'm too far gone, too weak, too broken. I may sit in darkness, but the Lord will be my light.

I declare that failure will not have the last word. Shame will not narrate my night. Regret will not steal my rest. You are not finished with me, and no mistake has cancelled Your promise. I silence the voice of despair and turn my ears to the song of hope You sing over me.

The enemy has no power to keep me in the place I fell. I rise in the name of Jesus. I sleep tonight in the arms of mercy. My weakness is not my identity. My night will be filled not with torment, but with testimony.

In Jesus' name, Amen.

Show

Your Voice Behind Me

> and when you turn to the right hand, and when you turn to the left, your ears will hear a voice behind you, saying, "This is the way. Walk in it."
> —Isaiah 30:21 WEB

Lord, I thank You that when I don't know where to turn, You are still speaking. You promised that whether I turn to the right or the left, I would hear Your voice behind me saying, "This is the way, walk in it." So tonight, I open my heart and spirit to that voice. Speak, even in the night.

As I sleep, let Your whisper guide me. If I am veering from the path, correct me with mercy. If I'm walking in fear, direct me back to faith. Give me clarity in the crossroads and calm in the chaos. Let Your Spirit teach me in the night hours, and let Your Word light the way.

I don't need to know every detail to move forward—I just need to hear You say, "This is the way." And I will follow. Lead me in dreams. Guide me with peace. Make Your direction undeniable. I will not wake confused but confident in Your guidance.

In Jesus' name, Amen.

SLEEP

RETURN TO REST, O MY SOUL

> Return to your rest, my soul, for Yahweh has dealt bountifully with you.
> —Psalms 116:7 WEB

Gracious Father, I speak to my own soul tonight: return to your rest, for the Lord has been good to you. You've delivered me from death, wiped the tears from my face, and steadied my feet on solid ground. What more do I need to lay down in peace? I have every reason to rest.

I let go of what I can't control and take hold of what I know—You are good. You are near. You are enough. I speak to the unrest in my chest and command it to settle. I speak to the swirling thoughts and command them to bow to peace. I do not need to strive—I simply need to trust.

Let this night be healing to my body, soothing to my mind, and refreshing to my spirit. I will wake not weary, but renewed. For I lay down in the promise that my Shepherd restores, my Father watches, and my soul is safe.

In Jesus' name, Amen.

DAY 14

SHUT

THE NAME THAT SEALS ME

> Yahweh's name is a strong tower: the righteous run to him, and are safe.
> —Proverbs 18:10 WEB

Strong Tower, I run into Your name tonight, and I am safe. I shut the door on every threat, every whisper of danger, and every shadow of fear. Your name is not just a word—it's a fortress. It surrounds me like impenetrable walls. I shut every spiritual gate tonight and mark them with the power of Your name, Jesus.

Let every assignment of the enemy be reversed by the authority of Your name. Let every plot fail before it reaches my door. No harm, no curse, no curse of night can prevail against the one who takes refuge in the Most High. I do not take shelter in superstition or chance—I am hidden in the name of the Lord.

I shut down access to the thief who comes to steal, kill, and destroy. The blood speaks better things. The name of Jesus is my seal. I sleep tonight knowing the power that protects me is greater than anything that rises against me.

In Jesus' name, Amen.

SHIELD

Held by His Hand

> For I, Yahweh your God, will hold your right hand, saying to you, 'Don't be afraid. I will help you.'
> —Isaiah 41:13 WEB

Abba Father, You said, "I am the Lord your God, who takes hold of your right hand and says to you, Do not fear; I will help you." Tonight, I place my hand in Yours. I do not face the dark alone. I do not navigate uncertainty in my own strength. You are with me, and You are holding me.

Let Your hand shield me from every scheme. Guard my heart from every blow. Keep me close when I feel surrounded. Even in the night, Your grip on me does not loosen. I am not slipping. I am not alone. I am not exposed. You are my covering and the lifter of my soul.

Wrap Your arm around my atmosphere. Send angels to stand beside my bed. Let Your grip be the wall that separates me from harm. I lie down as a child held by a loving Father, shielded by the strength of His everlasting arm.

In Jesus' name, Amen.

SILENCE

PEACE IN MY INNER STORM

> In the multitude of my thoughts within me, your comforts delight my soul.
> —Psalms 94:19 WEB

God of Comfort, in the multitude of my anxious thoughts, You bring me peace. Tonight, I silence every voice of worry and unrest. I shut down the chatter that keeps me tossing and turning. You are not the author of confusion, but of peace—and I welcome Your voice to speak louder than all the rest.

Quiet the "what ifs." Mute the "not enoughs." Still the replaying of the day's regrets and tomorrow's unknowns. I trade the storm in my mind for the stillness of Your presence. Let Your nearness blanket my heart. Let Your comfort fill the empty places where fear once lived.

I am not my own comforter—You are. And You never run out. Let peace flood my soul and calm the storm within. I am safe in the silence where only Your Spirit speaks.

In Jesus' name, Amen.

SHOW

LED BY THE SPIRIT OF TRUTH

> However when he, the Spirit of truth, has come, he will guide you into all truth, for he will not speak from himself; but whatever he hears, he will speak. He will declare to you things that are coming.
> —John 16:13 WEB

Holy Spirit, You are the Spirit of Truth, and You promised to guide me into all truth. Tonight, I lean into Your leading. As I sleep, lead me beyond confusion. Pull back the curtain on what's unclear. Speak in the night watches with clarity that can only come from heaven.

Reveal to me what's real and what's deception. Help me discern what's divine and what's distraction. Whisper the wisdom I need to navigate tomorrow. Show me the next step—even if it's just to wait. I don't ask to know it all; I ask to follow You faithfully.

Let truth rise in my spirit like the morning sun. Illuminate my heart with peace and purpose. While my body rests, let my spirit receive divine understanding. I declare that I will not walk in circles—I will walk in truth.

In Jesus' name, Amen.

SLEEP

DWELLING IN THE SECRET PLACE

> He who dwells in the secret place of the Most High will rest in the shadow of the Almighty. I will say of Yahweh, "He is my refuge and my fortress; my God, in whom I trust."
> —Psalms 91:1-2 WEB

Almighty God, I dwell tonight in the secret place of the Most High. I abide under the shadow of the Almighty. This is not symbolic—it is real. I am covered, hidden, and secure in the safety of Your presence. No fear can survive here. No terror of night can break in.

I say of the Lord: You are my refuge and my fortress. My God, in You I trust. I don't sleep in uncertainty—I sleep in faith. I don't lie down in dread—I lie down in covenant security. Your presence wraps around me like a warm blanket of protection and love.

Let this sleep be holy. Let it restore my body, reset my thoughts, and reignite my hope. I lay down in the place where no enemy can touch me and no anxiety can reach me. I will both lie down and sleep in peace—for You alone, O Lord, make me dwell in safety.

In Jesus' name, Amen.

DAY 15

SHUT

ENCAMPED BY HEAVEN'S HOST

> Yahweh's angel encamps around those who fear him, and delivers them.
> —Psalms 34:7 WEB

Lord of Hosts, I thank You tonight that the angel of the Lord encamps around those who fear You—and delivers them. I shut every door that darkness could attempt to creep through. No shadow can break through the encampment You have set around me. No curse can cross the border where angels stand guard. I declare tonight that my sleep is surrounded by the armies of heaven.

Let every gate be sealed with glory. Let every spiritual intruder be driven back. I do not rest in fear—I rest under divine surveillance. You are not only watching me; You've assigned angels to wage war on my behalf while I rest in peace. I trust in the unseen protection that surrounds me like a wall of fire.

I shut the gates to worry and dread. I close every opening to torment. I lie down under the covering of a heavenly encampment that never sleeps or fails.

In Jesus' name, Amen.

SHIELD

UNSHAKABLE AND UNMOVED

A Song of Ascents. Those who trust in Yahweh are as Mount Zion, which can't be moved, but remains forever.
—Psalms 125:1 WEB

Mighty God, tonight I rest as one who trusts in You. Your Word says those who trust in the Lord are like Mount Zion—unshakable, immovable, and forever secure. I take refuge in that truth. You are my shield, and because I stand in You, I cannot be toppled by the storms of life or the schemes of the enemy.

Let every attempt to rattle my soul be met with Your unmovable presence. Let every blow fall flat before Your shield. I am not tossed by every fear, not moved by every wind. I am grounded in grace and anchored in truth. I declare that no disturbance can shake the peace You've established in me tonight.

While the world trembles, I rest like a mountain in Your presence—stable, secure, and shielded by Your everlasting strength.

In Jesus' name, Amen.

SILENCE

THE ENEMY HAS BEEN DISARMED

> having stripped the principalities and the powers, he made a show of them openly, triumphing over them in it.
> —Colossians 2:15 WEB

Victorious Jesus, I thank You tonight that You have disarmed principalities and powers, triumphing over them by the cross. The enemy has already lost his voice of accusation, his tools of torment, and his grip of fear. So I silence every lying spirit, every suggestion of defeat, every sound of intimidation that tries to echo in the dark.

Let the cross be the final word. Let resurrection power shut the mouth of the accuser. I declare that I will not relive battles that have already been won. Satan has been stripped. His voice is void. His hold is broken. I sleep tonight not as a victim but as a victor—because Christ has overcome.

No voice from the pit will speak over me. No whisper of condemnation will define me. The silence of peace will reign in my room, for the roar of Calvary has spoken once and for all.

In Jesus' name, Amen.

Show

A Door Standing Open in Heaven

> After these things I looked and saw a door opened in heaven, and the first voice that I heard, like a trumpet speaking with me, was one saying, "Come up here, and I will show you the things which must happen after this."
> —Revelation 4:1 WEB

Holy Spirit, tonight I look up with expectation. Just as John saw a door standing open in heaven, I ask You to open a window of revelation over me. Show me what is on Your heart. Give me a glimpse of what is to come. While I sleep, open my spirit to the supernatural. Draw me into divine perspective.

I'm not satisfied with surface-level understanding. I long for heaven's insight. Reveal what lies beyond the next step. Speak what eyes haven't seen and ears haven't heard. Let me behold the higher things—things that elevate my thinking and enlarge my faith.

Draw me into deeper encounters as I rest. Unlock mysteries. Confirm direction. Show me the throne that governs all things, and remind me that I am seated with You in heavenly places. Let this be a night of heavenly perspective.

In Jesus' name, Amen.

SLEEP

After You Have Suffered a While

> But may the God of all grace, who called you to his eternal glory by Christ Jesus, after you have suffered a little while, perfect, establish, strengthen, and settle you.
> —1 Peter 5:10 WEB

Faithful God, tonight I rest in Your eternal promise: that after I have suffered a while, You will restore, confirm, strengthen, and establish me. I do not lie down defeated—I lie down being rebuilt. My pain is not permanent. My story is not over. My rest is the beginning of restoration.

I give You my bruises. I hand You my weariness. I lay down with hope, because You are not just letting time pass—You are working in the night. As I sleep, let strength return. Let healing flow. Let wholeness rise from every broken place.

You are perfecting me even as I rest. Let me wake up more rooted, more secure, more grounded in Your love. My sleep tonight is sacred—it is not escape, but preparation for glory.

In Jesus' name, Amen.

DAY 16

SHUT

MAKE THE CROOKED PLACES STRAIGHT

> "I will go before you, and make the rough places smooth. I will break the doors of brass in pieces, and cut apart the bars of iron.
> —Isaiah 45:2 WEB

Mighty God, I come into this night with the confidence that You go before me to make the crooked places straight. I shut every backdoor the enemy would try to twist into an open gate. I close off every detour, every false path, and every hidden snare designed to trip me in the dark. I declare that the way ahead—both natural and spiritual—is being cleared by Your power.

Let every barrier be shattered, and every spiritual ambush disarmed. Let hidden traps be exposed before they ever reach me. I rest tonight knowing that You are going ahead of me, removing obstacles, and leveling the ground. I do not fear the unknown, for the God of heaven is already moving on my behalf.

Tonight, I shut the door to confusion and sabotage. You are preparing a straight path for my feet, and I sleep with confidence that the way is already being made.

In Jesus' name, Amen.

Shield

A Stronghold in the Day of Trouble

> Yahweh is good, a stronghold in the day of trouble; and he knows those who take refuge in him.
> —Nahum 1:7 WEB

Lord, You are good—a refuge in the day of trouble. You know those who trust in You, and I declare tonight that I am known by You. You are not a distant shelter, but a present shield. As I lay down, I take comfort that I am surrounded by a refuge that cannot be shaken.

Let every arrow be caught by Your goodness. Let the fires of the enemy be extinguished before they reach my dwelling. Let no hidden danger overtake me in my sleep. I take my place beneath Your wings, shielded by mercy and kept by power. I will not fear the terror of the night, for my God is near.

While others run and hide, I remain still in the fortress of Your love. You are my place of safety, my stronghold, my ever-present help. You are the reason I can sleep in peace.

In Jesus' name, Amen.

Silence

Peace That Guards My Mind

> And the peace of God, which surpasses all understanding, will guard your hearts and your thoughts in Christ Jesus.
> —Philippians 4:7 WEB

Prince of Peace, tonight I surrender every anxious thought, every loud emotion, and every runaway fear to the authority of Your peace. You promised that Your peace, which surpasses all understanding, will guard my heart and mind in Christ Jesus. So I quiet my soul beneath Your shadow. Let peace be my shield and silence be my sanctuary.

I rebuke the noise of unrest and the clamor of doubt. I silence the fear of tomorrow and the regrets of today. Let nothing occupy my mind that has not passed through the filter of Your peace. Guard me from the war of my own thoughts. Protect my inner life from the storms of the outer world.

Tonight, let peace reign like a mighty river. Let it wash away every mental weight and emotional burden. I rest not because everything is solved, but because everything is surrendered.

In Jesus' name, Amen.

Show

I Will Speak in Visions

> He said, "Now hear my words. If there is a prophet among you, I, Yahweh, will make myself known to him in a vision. I will speak with him in a dream.
> —Numbers 12:6 WEB

Holy Spirit, You promised to make Yourself known in visions and speak in dreams. So I open my heart and my sleep to divine encounter. I long for more than rest—I long for revelation. Speak to me as I lie still. Show me what eyes cannot see and teach me what the day could not.

Let my sleep become sacred ground for encounter. Give me divine impressions, dreams soaked in truth, and visions aligned with Your Word. May every image, thought, or whisper from You bring clarity and confirmation. Remove the fog from my decisions and illuminate the hidden path ahead.

Tonight, I do not chase dreams—I welcome Your voice. Guide me in the night, and let the morning reveal that You were speaking all along.

In Jesus' name, Amen.

Sleep

Songs in the Night

> Yahweh will command his loving kindness in the daytime. In the night his song shall be with me: a prayer to the God of my life.
> —Psalms 42:8 WEB

Father, Your song will be with me in the night—a melody of mercy that carries me into peace. As the waves of the day settle and the room grows still, I listen for the song that only heaven can compose. Let the soundtrack of my sleep be the sound of Your faithfulness.

Sing over my tired soul. Hum over the worries I can't name. Wrap my dreams in harmonies of healing and hope. I rest tonight beneath a lullaby written by the Spirit—one that reminds me that You are near, You are good, and You are working in the unseen.

Let Your love be the rhythm that slows my breath and calms my chest. Let Your presence be the melody that holds me safe. I surrender this night to Your holy song and receive rest that renews, restores, and revives.

In Jesus' name, Amen.

DAY 17

SHUT

YOU ARE MY HIDING PLACE

> You are my hiding place. You will preserve me from trouble. You will surround me with songs of deliverance. Selah.
> —Psalms 32:7 WEB

Faithful Father, I run into the shelter of Your presence tonight. You are my hiding place—my shielded refuge from every trouble and hidden threat. I shut every spiritual doorway that would try to grant access to fear, torment, or distraction. I declare that no weapon, no whisper, no wandering spirit will find me, because I am hidden in You.

Let every attempt to track, trace, or trap me be confused and scattered by Your covering. You surround me with songs of deliverance—songs that shut the mouth of accusation and drown out every lie. I am not exposed in the night; I am covered in grace, sealed in the Spirit, and hidden in Christ.

I lie down knowing I'm not just protected—I am invisible to the enemy, because I am under divine concealment. Let the blood of Jesus be the mark that says: "Do not touch."

In Jesus' name, Amen.

SHIELD

FLAWLESS DEFENDER OF MY WAY

> As for God, his way is perfect. Yahweh's word is tried. He is a shield to all those who take refuge in him.
> —Psalms 18:30 WEB

Perfect God, Your way is blameless, and Your Word is flawless. Tonight, I rest under the perfection of Your protection. You are not only my God—you are my shield. You cover my weak points. You defend my blind spots. You are a fortress around me, and no adversary can penetrate the armor of Your truth.

I place my trust not in what I can see, but in who You are. The shield You provide is not made by human hands—it is forged by Your faithfulness. It blocks every unseen arrow and absorbs every fiery dart before it reaches me. I declare that I am guarded on all sides by the God whose way is perfect.

Though I don't know what the enemy has planned, I know who covers me—and that is enough. I rest beneath an unbreakable shield.

In Jesus' name, Amen.

SILENCE

HE WILL BLESS ME WITH PEACE

> Yahweh will give strength to his people. Yahweh will bless his people with peace.
> —Psalms 29:11 WEB

God of Glory, You thunder over the flood and speak in power, but You also bless Your people with peace. So tonight, I tune out the chaos and tune in to the quiet power of Your presence. I silence the inner storm. I bring every thought, every fear, every spinning worry into stillness before You.

You don't just calm the storm outside—I invite You to calm the one within. Let Your peace settle into the deepest places of unrest in me. Let every racing thought be subdued by the weight of Your glory. I refuse to allow noise to rule my night.

I declare tonight that peace is not the absence of trouble—it's the presence of God. And because You are near, I sleep under a blessing that cannot be broken: the blessing of peace.

In Jesus' name, Amen.

SHOW

I WILL STAND AND WATCH

> I will stand at my watch, and set myself on the ramparts, and will look out to see what he will say to me, and what I will answer concerning my complaint.
> —Habakkuk 2:1 WEB

Holy Spirit, tonight I take my place on the watchtower. I may be lying down in the natural, but in the Spirit, I am alert. I position myself to hear from You—to wait and watch for what You will say. I invite You to reveal the things that eyes cannot see and ears have not yet heard.

As I sleep, let my spirit remain attentive. If You desire to speak in dreams, I am open. If You choose to instruct in the night, I am listening. I watch not with fear but with expectation. I trust You to answer questions I've carried too long, to bring light where I've sat in shadows.

Tonight, let me hear You clearly. Let me see beyond the moment. Give me vision for the season ahead, even while I sleep. I am on watch, and You are speaking.

In Jesus' name, Amen.

SLEEP

I Lay Down and Slept

> I laid myself down and slept. I awakened; for Yahweh sustains me.
> —Psalms 3:5 WEB

Gracious Lord, I lay down tonight with peace in my soul, because You sustained me. I didn't make it through today by my own strength—it was Your hand that carried me. So now, I release my body, mind, and spirit into Your keeping. I will sleep, not just as one who is tired, but as one who trusts.

Let sleep come swiftly and sweetly. Let every muscle relax under the weight of Your presence. Let my breath slow as my spirit sinks deeper into rest. I refuse to carry into the night what You've already handled in the day.

I lay down and sleep because You are awake. I rest because You never do. I trust You to restore, renew, and prepare me for tomorrow. My rest tonight is a declaration: I am kept by the Lord.

In Jesus' name, Amen.

DAY 18

SHUT

PRESERVED FROM THE HANDS OF THE WICKED

> Yahweh, keep me from the hands of the wicked. Preserve me from the violent men who have determined to trip my feet.
> —Psalms 140:4 WEB

Lord, my Defender, tonight I shut the doors of my life to every wicked plot and evil hand stretched out against me. You are the One who delivers me from the power of the violent. I close the gates to sabotage, betrayal, and every covert work of darkness. No wicked hand will touch what You have covered.

Preserve me, O Lord, from hidden dangers and spiritual traps. Let every assignment sent to harm me fall powerless. I seal the atmosphere of my home and mind with the authority of Christ. The hands of the wicked are bound. The schemes of the violent are scattered. I lie down in safety, knowing You have fenced me in with holy fire.

Tonight, I declare that no plan formed against me shall prevail. You are my refuge, and in You, I am untouchable by the wicked.

In Jesus' name, Amen.

SHIELD

ANGELS ON ASSIGNMENT

> For he will put his angels in charge of you, to guard you in all your ways.
> —Psalms 91:11 WEB

Father, I praise You for Your faithful promise—You have commanded Your angels concerning me, to guard me in all my ways. Tonight, I release heaven's hosts over my life. Let every angel assigned to my dwelling, my family, and my destiny take their place in strength. I am not alone; I am surrounded.

Shield me from what I cannot see. Deflect every dart, divert every ambush, and guard every spiritual gate. Let no harm come near. I invoke the divine shield of angelic protection to cover the night hours. Let heaven's warriors encircle my home like a wall of fire and light.

I do not rest in fear but in full assurance that Your angels are executing their charge. Their swords are drawn, their wings are spread, and their watch is constant.

In Jesus' name, Amen.

SILENCE

WHY ARE YOU AFRAID?

He said to them, "Why are you fearful, O you of little faith?"
Then he got up, rebuked the wind and the sea, and there was
a great calm.
—Matthew 8:26 WEB

Lord Jesus, You speak peace to storms with a word. So tonight, I surrender every fear—fear of harm, fear of the unknown, fear of the what-ifs—and I listen for Your voice above the chaos. You ask, "Why are you afraid?" And I answer with trust: I believe You are here.

I silence the winds of worry and rebuke the waves of anxiety. I command fear to be still. I speak quietness over my thoughts and confidence over my emotions. You are not absent in the storm—you are in the boat, and that changes everything.

So I speak peace over the storm within me and around me. Fear has no foothold. I rest because the One who controls the sea is watching over me.

In Jesus' name, Amen.

SHOW

DREAMS AND VISIONS IN THE NIGHT

> 'It will be in the last days, says God, that I will pour out my Spirit on all flesh. Your sons and your daughters will prophesy. Your young men will see visions. Your old men will dream dreams.
> —Acts 2:17 WEB

Spirit of God, pour Yourself out tonight. Your Word promises that in the last days, You will speak through dreams and visions. I receive that promise tonight with open hands and a ready heart. As I lie down to rest, I invite heaven to speak. Let my dreams be filled with divine instruction, insight, and revelation.

Reveal what You are doing. Show me what's ahead. Unfold hidden truths, confirm Your word, and open the eyes of my understanding. Let the night be filled with whispers from heaven and visions that awaken purpose. I long not for entertainment, but encounter.

Tonight, I yield my sleep to You, Holy Spirit. Visit me in the night watches and release the clarity I need. May I rise not only refreshed, but illuminated by what You've shown me.

In Jesus' name, Amen.

Sleep

I Will Heal You in Rest

'Behold, I will bring it health and cure, and I will cure them; and I will reveal to them abundance of peace and truth.
—Jeremiah 33:6 WEB

Healer of my soul, I lay down tonight in full expectation—not just of sleep, but of healing. You promised to bring health and healing, to restore and revive. So I surrender my body, mind, and emotions into Your care. Let the balm of heaven flow over every ache and weariness.

Where there has been strain—release it. Where there has been heaviness—lift it. Where I've felt depleted—renew me. Let this night be a holy exchange: my exhaustion for Your restoration, my tension for Your tenderness, my brokenness for Your mending hand.

I sleep under the shadow of the Healer. Let every system in my body come into alignment. Let peace flood every troubled place. When I rise, I will rise whole, restored, and revived.

In Jesus' name, Amen.

DAY 19

SHUT

THEY SHALL NOT PREVAIL

> They will fight against you, but they will not prevail against you; for I am with you", says Yahweh, "to rescue you."
> —Jeremiah 1:19 WEB

Almighty God, I thank You tonight that though adversaries may rise against me, they shall not prevail. I shut every access point the enemy would use to launch attacks while I sleep. I silence every rising force of darkness and cancel every word, weapon, and scheme designed to unseat my peace. They may fight, but they will fail—because You are with me.

I place my spirit, body, and space under divine lockdown. Let every evil intention crumble before it begins. Let confusion overtake those who plot evil in the night. I shut every gate of fear, harassment, and retaliation in the name of Jesus.

Tonight, I lie down unafraid. For though the battle rages, You are the God who has already spoken: they shall not overcome me.

In Jesus' name, Amen.

SHIELD

UNDERNEATH ARE EVERLASTING ARMS

> The eternal God is your dwelling place. Underneath are the everlasting arms. He thrust out the enemy from before you, and said, 'Destroy!'
> —Deuteronomy 33:27 WEB

Father, I rest tonight in the security of Your everlasting arms. You are my refuge—the eternal God who carries me when I am weary and shields me when I am vulnerable. I am not left to defend myself. I am held, supported, and covered by strength that never runs dry.

Wrap me in Your arms, Lord. Let every fiery dart be quenched by Your presence. Let every evil force trying to reach me find only You—my unshakable defense. You lift me above danger and carry me through the dark. I fear no evil, for Your arms surround me.

I release every burden and lean into the arms that never fail. Tonight, I do not brace myself—I rest myself in You.

In Jesus' name, Amen.

SILENCE

TAKE EVERY THOUGHT CAPTIVE

> throwing down imaginations and every high thing that is exalted against the knowledge of God, and bringing every thought into captivity to the obedience of Christ;
> —2 Corinthians 10:5 WEB

God of Truth, tonight I submit my mind to You. I bring every rogue thought, every anxious loop, every lie from the pit into captivity. I silence the mental noise that keeps me restless and declare that only Your truth will echo in my soul. I cast down imaginations and arguments that try to exalt themselves above Your peace.

No fear shall dominate this night. No inner accusation shall win. I take authority over the battlefield of my mind, and I declare it a sanctuary of stillness. Let every unclean voice be silenced. Let every tormenting replay be shut down. I set my thoughts on You—pure, perfect, and true.

Tonight, I lay my head not just on a pillow, but on Your promises. My thoughts are guarded, my mind is sound, and my sleep will be safe.

In Jesus' name, Amen.

Show

In Your Light, I See Light

> For with you is the spring of life. In your light shall we see light.
> —Psalms 36:9 WEB

Father of Light, I turn my face toward You tonight, asking that You would illuminate my soul. In Your light, I see light—truth, perspective, wisdom, and revelation. Open my eyes in the Spirit. Let me perceive what cannot be seen by the natural mind.

Show me what decisions need clarity. Reveal where I've walked in shadows. Let the light of Your presence make the unclear obvious and the crooked path straight. Speak in the night through images, dreams, impressions, and divine insight. I am not groping for guidance—I'm gazing into glory.

As I rest, shine Your light into every part of my being. Flood my spirit with the radiance of Your wisdom. When I wake, let it be with vision that only You could provide.

In Jesus' name, Amen.

Sleep

The Keeper Who Never Sleeps

> He will not allow your foot to be moved. He who keeps you will not slumber. Behold, he who keeps Israel will neither slumber nor sleep.
> —Psalms 121:3-4 WEB

Faithful Watchman, You never sleep nor slumber. And because You stay awake, I can truly rest. I lay down tonight with full assurance that You are keeping watch over me—not just passively, but actively guarding every detail of my life. You are my Keeper.

Let nothing slip past Your gaze. Let no harm approach without being stopped by Your presence. I sleep without fear because the night belongs to You. My rest is not vulnerable—it is covered by the One who sees everything and misses nothing.

As I close my eyes, I give up the need to watch over myself. You've got me. You always have. I will lie down and sleep in peace, for You alone, O Lord, make me dwell in safety.

In Jesus' name, Amen.

DAY 20

SHUT

WHOM SHALL I FEAR?

By David. Yahweh is my light and my salvation. Whom shall I fear? Yahweh is the strength of my life. Of whom shall I be afraid? When evildoers came at me to eat up my flesh, even my adversaries and my foes, they stumbled and fell. Though an army should encamp against me, my heart shall not fear. Though war should rise against me, even then I will be confident.
—Psalms 27:1-3 WEB

Lord, my Light and my Salvation, whom shall I fear? Tonight, I shut the doors of dread and bolt the gates against every threat that rises in the dark. Though war may rise against me, my heart will not be afraid. I dwell in safety because You dwell with me.

I declare that fear has no access to my night. I shut down every spirit of intimidation and every lie that exaggerates my weakness. You are the stronghold of my life—nothing can breach the walls You've established. Let every evil plot be dismantled before it unfolds. Let every night terror dissolve under the light of Your glory.

I sleep as one who is confident in her Defender, and I declare that no force in hell can overpower the one who trusts in the Lord.

In Jesus' name, Amen.

SHIELD

THE LORD IS MY STRENGTH

> Yah is my strength and song. He has become my salvation.
> —Psalms 118:14 WEB

Almighty God, You are my strength and my song. You have become my salvation. I rest beneath the shield of Your power tonight—not in my own resilience, but in Your everlasting strength. You are the reason I can breathe easy, the reason I can close my eyes without fear.

Shield me from emotional weariness and mental fatigue. Guard me from despair and inner collapse. I will not cave under the weight of the day because You are lifting me. You are the power behind my praise and the anchor beneath my rest.

Tonight, let Your strength surround me like a wall that cannot be moved. I lie down in joy, because the joy of the Lord is my strength.

In Jesus' name, Amen.

Silence

Redeemed From the Battle

> He has redeemed my soul in peace from the battle that was against me, although there are many who oppose me.
> —Psalms 55:18 WEB

Redeeming Lord, You rescue my soul in peace from the battle that raged against me. So tonight, I speak peace over every place of internal warfare. I silence the noise of regret, guilt, and fear. I declare an end to the inner striving and invite Your voice to be the only one that speaks.

You are not only the One who saves—I declare You as the One who stills. You redeem the war-torn places in my spirit. You silence the tormentor and still the storm. Let the clash of voices be silenced. Let the shouting of condemnation be drowned out by Your mercy.

Tonight, I sleep as one who has been rescued. The battle is not mine—it belongs to You. And You have already won.

In Jesus' name, Amen.

SHOW

YOU REVEAL DEEP THINGS

> He uncovers deep things out of darkness, and brings out to light the shadow of death.
> —Job 12:22 WEB

O God, You reveal deep and hidden things. Tonight, I ask You to speak to me beyond what I can reach on my own. While I sleep, uncover what has been concealed. Pull back the curtain on decisions, direction, and mysteries that linger in the shadows of my heart.

Shine Your light on what I've been too busy to notice. Bring wisdom where I've hit a wall. I don't want surface answers—I long for deep revelation. Let Your voice cut through confusion and lift me into divine perspective. Let dreams carry meaning, and visions bring instruction.

As I lie still, let there be movement in the Spirit. I trust that while I rest, You reveal. While I sleep, You speak. I will awaken with answers because the God of mystery is near.

In Jesus' name, Amen.

Sleep

Held by His Embrace

> His left hand is under my head. His right hand embraces me.
> —Song of Solomon 2:6 WEB

Jesus, tonight I rest in the embrace of Your love. Your left hand is under my head, and Your right hand embraces me. I am not falling into sleep—I am being held. I surrender to the safety of Your arms and let go of the day, knowing I am wrapped in everlasting love.

Let Your embrace quiet every anxious breath. Let Your nearness soften every tight place in my chest. I do not drift—I am carried. I do not collapse—I am caught. Let this night be filled with sacred stillness and divine affection. I am loved, I am known, I am safe.

Hold me close until the morning light. And when I wake, let me rise still held by You.

In Jesus' name, Amen.

DAY 21

SHUT

THE HEAVENS FIGHT FOR ME

> From the sky the stars fought. From their courses, they fought against Sisera.
> —Judges 5:20 WEB

Lord of Hosts, tonight I rest knowing that the heavens themselves fight on my behalf. Just as the stars fought in their courses in the days of Deborah, so now the forces of heaven rise to war for me. I shut every earthly and demonic gate that opposes what You have ordained. I declare tonight that I am not outnumbered—I am backed by glory.

Every enemy that refuses to bow to Your will must contend not just with me, but with the armies of the Lord. I close access to retaliation, counterattack, and backlash. I seal every opening the enemy might exploit. The battle is not mine—it belongs to You, and the heavens are engaged.

Let the invisible realms align with Your word over my life. Let principalities be displaced and territorial strongholds be overthrown. I am not vulnerable; I am under divine strategy and covered by holy warfare. As I sleep, war in the heavenlies. Let the victory be established before the morning light.

In Jesus' name, Amen.

SHIELD

Rescued and Surrounded

> The righteous cry, and Yahweh hears, and delivers them out of all their troubles.
> —Psalms 34:17 WEB

Faithful Deliverer, when the righteous cry out, You hear and deliver them from all their troubles. Tonight, I lift my voice to You—not in panic, but in confidence that You will surround me with rescue. You are not far off; You are near to those whose hearts are crushed. I take shelter under the wings of Your deliverance tonight.

Shield me from every trouble I can see—and every one I cannot. Let angelic rescue missions be released in the night to pull me out of traps I didn't even know were set. Let the shield of favor surround me as with a wall. Let every unseen enemy stumble at the edge of the hedge You've built around me.

I do not sleep as one in danger, but as one preserved. I do not lie down alone—I am encircled. You've promised to deliver me from all my troubles, and even in the night hours, that promise still stands.

In Jesus' name, Amen.

SILENCE

KEYS TO LOCK AND LOOSE

> I will give to you the keys of the Kingdom of Heaven, and whatever you bind on earth will have been bound in heaven; and whatever you release on earth will have been released in heaven."
> —Matthew 16:19 WEB

Sovereign Jesus, You've given me the keys of the Kingdom, and tonight I use them in faith. I silence every unauthorized voice by locking the gates of access to my mind, body, and spirit. I shut the door to torment, unrest, and disturbance, and I loose peace, clarity, and divine stillness over this night.

I bind confusion and loose divine order. I bind fear and loose boldness. I bind sleeplessness and loose rest. I declare that what is bound on earth is bound in heaven, and what is loosed on earth is loosed in heaven. My words are not empty—they echo heaven's authority.

Let no voice of the accuser speak tonight. Let no spirit of heaviness or oppression linger in my space. I take back the airwaves of my mind and declare them subject to the rule of Christ. The gates of hell will not prevail against the sleep You've ordained for me.

In Jesus' name, Amen.

SHOW

SPEAK, LORD—I'M LISTENING

> Yahweh came, and stood, and called as at other times, "Samuel! Samuel!" Then Samuel said, "Speak; for your servant hears."
> —1 Samuel 3:10 WEB

Holy Spirit, tonight I posture my heart like Samuel and say: "Speak, Lord, for Your servant is listening." I don't just want to hear words—I want to hear Your voice. I open my spirit to divine communication, even while I rest. Let the ears of my soul be alert, even in sleep.

If You whisper, I will hear. If You give vision, I will receive. I silence the noise within so I can perceive what You are saying. Let this night be holy—set apart for intimacy with You. Let my dreams be filled with meaning, and my rest be rich with revelation.

Show me the next step. Unveil what I've missed. Clarify what I've questioned. I trust You not only to speak—but to help me discern. I don't want to wake up the same. I want to rise changed, aligned, and assured by Your voice.

In Jesus' name, Amen.

SLEEP

REMEMBERING YOU IN THE NIGHT

> My soul shall be satisfied as with the richest food. My mouth shall praise you with joyful lips, when I remember you on my bed, and think about you in the night watches.
> —Psalms 63:5-6 WEB

God of my life, I remember You on my bed. I meditate on You in the night watches. Tonight, I don't fall asleep distracted—I fall asleep in devotion. As I close my eyes, I fix them on Your goodness. I quiet my heart in the awareness of Your love.

Let my thoughts return to every place You've rescued me, every moment You've spoken peace, every time You've carried me. You have never failed me. And tonight, I reflect on that faithfulness. I do not rehearse the day's chaos—I rehearse Your covenant.

Let this meditation stir up peace within me. Let it still my emotions and slow my breath. I sleep not because I forget my troubles, but because I remember my God. You are the reason I can let go. You are the reason I will wake up whole.

In Jesus' name, Amen.

DAY 22

SHUT

HIDDEN IN THE SHELTER

> In the shelter of your presence you will hide them from the plotting of man. You will keep them secretly in a dwelling away from the strife of tongues.
> —Psalms 31:20 WEB

Father, I thank You that You hide me in the secret place of Your presence from the conspiracies of men. Tonight, I shut every spiritual window, gate, and door that would attempt to expose me to danger, fear, or attack. I declare that I am not vulnerable—I am hidden. Let every evil plan, slanderous word, or demonic surveillance be utterly silenced and scattered. I do not rest in the open; I am tucked away in the shelter of the Most High.

Hide me, Lord, from emotional ambush, spiritual manipulation, and the toxic agendas of others. You are my covering and my concealment. You preserve my life from trouble and surround me with songs of deliverance. I shut the gate to anxiety, to panic, and to emotional fatigue. I am sealed in Your peace.

Tonight, I sleep beneath Your shadow. I do not wrestle; I rest. I do not fear; I am hidden.

In Jesus' name, Amen.

SHIELD

THE CRY OF THE OPPRESSED

> "Because of the oppression of the weak and because of the groaning of the needy, I will now arise," says Yahweh; "I will set him in safety from those who malign him."
> —Psalms 12:5 WEB

Delivering God, You have seen the affliction of Your people. You hear the groaning of those pressed down and worn thin. And You arise. Tonight, I cry out—not from despair, but from faith. I know that You will lift me up and surround me with protection. Shield me from the pressures that threaten to crush my peace. Let the groaning of my soul rise as a prayer You will not ignore.

Protect me from what people say and do in secret. Be my Defender in conversations I will never hear. Be my Advocate in places I cannot go. Let the injustice I've carried break under the weight of Your intervention. Let every invisible burden be shattered by the shield of Your presence.

You will place me in safety, far from the reach of torment. I rest tonight not just defended, but deeply cared for by the God who sees and responds.

In Jesus' name, Amen.

SILENCE

YOU STILL THE ROARING

> By awesome deeds of righteousness, you answer us, God of our salvation. You who are the hope of all the ends of the earth, of those who are far away on the sea; Who by his power forms the mountains, having armed yourself with strength; who stills the roaring of the seas, the roaring of their waves, and the turmoil of the nations.
> —Psalms 65:5-7 WEB

Lord, You are the One who stills the roaring of the seas, the roaring of their waves, and the turmoil of the nations. So tonight, still the roaring within me. Quiet the turbulence of unanswered questions, silent pain, and underlying tension. I release to You every emotion that's grown too loud, every thought crashing like waves against my soul.

Silence the voice of regret. Still the noise of comparison. Quench the fiery darts of doubt. I refuse to carry mental chaos into my rest. I will not toss and turn while You are on the throne. You don't just calm the oceans—you calm me.

Let Your peace act as a holy hush over my mind. I am still now. Not because the world has stopped spinning—but because You hold it, and You hold me.

In Jesus' name, Amen.

SHOW

STEPS DIRECTED BY THE LORD

> Counsel in the heart of man is like deep water; but a man of understanding will draw it out.
> —Proverbs 20:5 WEB

Lord, Your Word says that a person's steps are directed by You—so tonight I rest, not in confusion, but in confidence. Even when I don't understand what's next, I know You are leading. I ask You now to show me what my eyes cannot see. As I lie down, open the unseen path and give me clarity where I've only had questions.

Let dreams come like arrows of precision. Let divine insight flow into my spirit. Reveal the wisdom I didn't know I needed and point my feet in the right direction. I am not leaning on my understanding; I'm leaning on Your guidance.

Even in the night, let my spirit walk with You. Settle the decisions I've been agonizing over. Bring clarity in the stillness. I trust that while I sleep, You are orchestrating every step I'll take when I rise.

In Jesus' name, Amen.

SLEEP

WATERED IN THE WILDERNESS

and Yahweh will guide you continually, and satisfy your soul in dry places, and make your bones strong; and you shall be like a watered garden, and like a spring of water, whose waters don't fail.
—Isaiah 58:11 WEB

Loving Shepherd, tonight I surrender to Your promise: You will guide me continually and satisfy my soul in drought. You will make me like a well-watered garden, like a spring whose waters never fail. I release the dryness of the day and open myself to the refreshing of Your Spirit.

Let my sleep tonight be a holy watering. Let Your presence restore every parched place, every depleted thought, every tired emotion. Breathe on me as I lie still. Let rivers flow through the cracks of weariness and bring new life. I will not wake up empty—I will wake up replenished.

Where I've been drained, fill me. Where I've been confused, center me. Where I've been striving, still me. I sleep now in the garden of Your grace, trusting that You are cultivating restoration in every part of me.

In Jesus' name, Amen.

DAY 23

SHUT

THE BREAKER HAS GONE BEFORE

> He who breaks open the way goes up before them. They break through the gate, and go out. And their king passes on before them, with Yahweh at their head.
> —Micah 2:13 WEB

O God, my Breaker, I thank You that You have gone before me. You lead the way through every barrier, obstruction, and spiritual blockade. Tonight, I shut every gate of resistance that has stood against my progress. I declare that every stronghold trying to hold me back is shattered by the power of the One who breaks open the path.

I seal off access to old cycles that try to return. I close the gate to sabotage and delay. The Breaker has already passed through, and because of that, I will not be stopped. Let the doors You've opened remain open, and let the ones You've shut never be reopened. I am not stuck—I am stepping forward, even in my sleep.

Tonight, I lie down not wondering how it will happen—I rest knowing the way has already been made.

In Jesus' name, Amen.

Shield

Singing Through the Night

> But I will sing of your strength. Yes, I will sing aloud of your loving kindness in the morning. For you have been my high tower, a refuge in the day of my distress.
> —Psalms 59:16 WEB

Faithful Deliverer, I will sing of Your strength tonight—I will lift a quiet song even in the shadows. You are my fortress, my refuge in times of trouble. Though the night may seem long, I am not alone. You are with me, shielding me, sustaining me, surrounding me.

Let Your song be my covering. Let the melody of Your mercy drown out every whisper of fear. Let Your presence stand like a wall between me and every ambush of the enemy. You are not only near in the morning; You are the God of my night.

I rejoice in the truth that I'm not waiting for a rescue—my Rescuer already reigns. You shield me as I sleep. I am wrapped in love and guarded by grace.

In Jesus' name, Amen.

SILENCE

BE SILENT, AND COME OUT

> Jesus rebuked him, saying, "Be quiet, and come out of him!"
> —Mark 1:25 WEB

Jesus, just as You spoke to the unclean spirit and commanded it to be silent and come out, I declare that same authority tonight over every voice that seeks to torment, deceive, or oppress. I silence every spirit that does not confess You as Lord. I drive out every presence that disturbs my rest or clouds my mind.

Let no voice rise in accusation. Let no word contrary to truth find space in my mind. I command silence to every whisper of fear, shame, or condemnation. This night belongs to the Spirit of God—no counterfeit voice is welcome here.

Your Word is final. Your peace is permanent. I take authority over the atmosphere and declare that every tongue lifted against me in judgment is condemned. Peace, be still. Silence, be restored.

In Jesus' name, Amen.

Show

He Made Known His Ways

> He made known his ways to Moses, his deeds to the children of Israel.
> —Psalms 103:7 WEB

God of Revelation, I thank You tonight that You make known not just Your acts—but Your ways. I'm not just seeking results—I'm seeking relationship. Show me Your patterns. Reveal Your heart. Let me understand how You move so I can walk with You more fully.

As I sleep, unfold the unseen. Let dreams speak of deeper things. Let the night hours bring understanding that daylight has not. I long to know You—not only for what You do, but for who You are. Reveal Yourself to me in the quiet of the night.

Let this be a night of communion. Pull me closer into Your counsel. Let wisdom arise, let direction become clear, and let intimacy deepen. I am open to Your ways, Your will, and Your whispers.

In Jesus' name, Amen.

Sleep

Faithfulness in the Night

> *A Psalm. A song for the Sabbath day.* It is a good thing to give thanks to Yahweh, to sing praises to your name, Most High; to proclaim your loving kindness in the morning, and your faithfulness every night,
> —Psalms 92:1-2 WEB

Faithful One, tonight I rest in the rhythm of Your goodness. It is good to declare Your steadfast love in the morning and Your faithfulness at night. So as I lie down, I reflect on every place You've come through—every moment You've kept me, every time You've lifted me.

Your faithfulness is not a feeling—it's a fact. You were faithful today, and You will be faithful tomorrow. So I release the need to control, understand, or resolve. I sleep under the banner of a faithful God.

Let Your constancy calm me. Let the certainty of Your nature settle every anxious place in me. I lay down tonight in the remembrance of Your goodness and rise tomorrow to fresh mercy again.

In Jesus' name, Amen.

DAY 24

SHUT

THE NAME THAT DEFENDS ME

For the Chief Musician. A Psalm by David. May Yahweh answer you in the day of trouble. May the name of the God of Jacob set you up on high,
—Psalms 20:1 WEB

O Lord, my Helper and Defender, I thank You that when I call on Your name, You answer me in the day of trouble. Tonight, I shut every doorway the enemy would try to use to bring trouble into my night. I declare that no distress, no demonic disturbance, and no spiritual backlash will rise against me in the secret hours. Your name is my refuge, and I run into it with confidence.

Let every opposing voice be silenced by the authority of Jesus' name. Let every dark agenda be dismantled before it reaches my home. I am not exposed to the night—I am covered by the power of the One whose name shakes heaven and earth. I shut down torment, fear, confusion, and unrest. I am defended by a name that never loses power.

Tonight, I sleep under the banner of the name of the Lord. Let every force that rises against me fall before that name.

In Jesus' name, Amen.

SHIELD

OUR SOUL WAITS FOR THE LORD

> Our soul has waited for Yahweh. He is our help and our shield.
> —Psalms 33:20 WEB

Faithful God, my soul waits for You tonight—not in anxiety, but in expectancy. You are my help and my shield. I do not rely on my own strength to guard me in the dark; I rely on You. You watch over my thoughts, protect my body, and defend my dwelling.

Shield me from unseen warfare and internal unrest. Let every fiery arrow of fear, doubt, or spiritual distraction be intercepted by Your presence. I raise my faith like a shield and declare: no threat will breach the hedge You have built around me. You are the watchman over my soul.

Tonight, I rest beneath divine security. I sleep not in fear, but in waiting—waiting on the God who never fails to show up.

In Jesus' name, Amen.

SILENCE

ABOVE ALL, TAKE THE SHIELD

> above all, taking up the shield of faith, with which you will be able to quench all the fiery darts of the evil one.
> —Ephesians 6:16 WEB

Mighty God, You have armed me with the shield of faith to quench every flaming dart of the evil one. So tonight, I lift that shield against every lie, every accusation, and every tormenting voice that seeks to disturb my rest. I silence every demonic suggestion with the authority of faith in Christ.

Faith speaks louder than fear. Faith drowns out shame. Faith extinguishes the fiery arrows of anxiety and doubt. I will not be moved by the noise in the night. I will not be shaken by the shadows. I lift my shield, and I silence the storm.

Let my faith in Your Word serve as a force field around my thoughts. Let Your truth guard the borders of my peace. Tonight, I am not defenseless—I am fully covered.

In Jesus' name, Amen.

SHOW

REVEALING THE HIDDEN MYSTERIES

> the mystery which has been hidden for ages and generations. But now it has been revealed to his saints,
> —Colossians 1:26 WEB

God of glory, I thank You that You are revealing the mystery that was hidden for ages—but now made known to those who seek. Tonight, I enter into that divine unveiling. I quiet my heart before You and ask that You would reveal things hidden, things deeper than intellect, and truths I need to see in this season.

Let my dreams be full of spiritual wisdom. Let divine patterns unfold while I rest. Uncover the direction that has been concealed. Show me the answer I didn't know how to ask for. Let the mystery become a message. Let the questions find holy answers in the watches of the night.

You are not a God who hides truth from me; You hide it for me—so that in intimacy, I may discover it. Tonight, I rest in the unveiling.

In Jesus' name, Amen.

SLEEP

YOU ARE WITH ME IN THE WATERS

> When you pass through the waters, I will be with you; and through the rivers, they will not overflow you. When you walk through the fire, you will not be burned, and flame will not scorch you.
> —Isaiah 43:2 WEB

Ever-present Lord, I rest tonight with this confidence: when I pass through the waters, You are with me. When I lie down in the deep stillness of night, You are beside me. I am not alone in the dark. You walk with me through the rivers of pressure, and You guard me when the fires of the day have tried to scorch my peace.

Tonight, I surrender the weight of what I've walked through. I release the residue of stress and battle. I let go of the burdens that clung to me from today. And I receive the promise that no river will sweep me away, and no flame will consume me.

Let Your presence be the cool in the fire and the calm in the flood. As I sleep, surround me with Your nearness. My soul is anchored by Your word, and my body will lie down in peace.

In Jesus' name, Amen.

DAY 25

SHUT

No Chaos, No Chase

> For you shall not go out in haste, neither shall you go by flight: for Yahweh will go before you; and the God of Israel will be your rear guard.
> —Isaiah 52:12 WEB

Lord, my Rear Guard, I thank You that I do not enter this night in haste or fear. You go before me, and You also come behind. Tonight, I shut every gate that leads to restlessness, panic, or emotional pursuit. I will not be chased by the stress of today or the worries of tomorrow. I seal the door to anxiety and declare peace over the corridors of my spirit.

I cancel every assignment of chaos meant to follow me into the night. I shut down the aftershocks of hurried conversations, tense moments, or unresolved emotions. You are not the author of confusion, but of calm. I lie down in a sacred stillness, protected by Your presence and led by Your peace.

Tonight, I declare: no emergency will erupt, no unseen trap will spring, and no spiritual ambush will prevail. I shut every gate the enemy might exploit. I am not vulnerable—I am defended.

In Jesus' name, Amen.

Shield

Your Gentleness Makes Me Great

> You have also given me the shield of your salvation. Your right hand sustains me. Your gentleness has made me great.
> —Psalms 18:35 WEB

Gracious God, You have stooped down to make me great. Tonight, I rest beneath the shield of Your gentleness. In a world that often bruises and batters, You cover me with tender strength. You enlarge the path beneath me so my feet will not slip. You protect me not only with might—but with mercy.

Shield me from harsh words, emotional weight, and the bruising blows of the day. Let Your gentleness wrap around me like a blanket of rest. I do not have to be strong tonight—You are strong for me. Let the softness of Your Spirit soothe the places that have been scraped by pressure or weariness.

You make room for me to breathe. You slow the pace so I can recover. Tonight, I am not bracing myself—I am leaning into grace.

In Jesus' name, Amen.

Silence

My Soul Is Quieted

Surely I have stilled and quieted my soul, like a weaned child with his mother, like a weaned child is my soul within me.
—Psalms 131:2 WEB

Father, I come before You tonight like a weaned child with its mother—my soul is quieted within me. I silence every inner protest, every cry for control, and every demand to figure it all out. I bring my soul under submission to peace. I cast off the heaviness of striving and let contentment rise like a holy hush.

Let every noisy memory, every spiraling thought, and every mental distraction be subdued by Your calm. I will not overanalyze today. I will not rehearse what went wrong. I receive rest as an act of worship. I do not need to know everything—only that You are here.

Tonight, I choose quiet over chaos. I settle my heart in Your nearness. Let stillness be my portion and serenity my inheritance.

In Jesus' name, Amen.

SHOW

EYES OPEN IN THE NIGHT

> My eyes stay open through the night watches, that I might meditate on your word.
> —Psalms 119:148 WEB

God of the night watches, while others sleep through the darkness, my eyes stay open—waiting for Your Word. I am not wide awake with worry, but with wonder. Speak to me, Lord. Reveal what You desire to say in the silence. Your Word is my meditation, and I long for its light to break into my spirit.

Unfold mysteries, whisper strategies, and release insight for the days ahead. I do not need another distraction—I need divine direction. Let the Scriptures come alive as I rest. Let night visions arise from the pages You have written for me.

As my body settles, let my spirit receive. I am alert to heaven. I am listening for You. You have my attention, even in sleep.

In Jesus' name, Amen.

SLEEP

Tomorrow Will Worry for Itself

> Therefore don't be anxious for tomorrow, for tomorrow will be anxious for itself. Each day's own evil is sufficient.
> —Matthew 6:34 WEB

Faithful Provider, I cast every care before You. I release tomorrow into Your hands. Tonight, I lay down all the "what ifs" and "what thens" and choose to rest in the sufficiency of today's grace. I will not borrow anxiety from a day I haven't yet lived. I will not lie awake rehearsing tomorrow's needs.

You have given me this night as a gift—not a burden. Let my body relax, my mind be still, and my soul exhale. You've promised that each day has its own provision, so I will not carry what doesn't belong to me yet. You are already in my tomorrow.

Tonight, I embrace the gift of now. I rest deeply. I sleep freely. I trust fully.

In Jesus' name, Amen.

DAY 26

SHUT

REFUGE IN THE MIDST OF TROUBLE

For the Chief Musician. By the sons of Korah. According to Alamoth. God is our refuge and strength, a very present help in trouble.
—Psalms 46:1 WEB

God, my Refuge and Strength, ever-present in trouble, I come into this night knowing I am not exposed. I shut every spiritual gate to panic, disaster, and disruption. Even if the earth gives way or the mountains shake, You remain unmoved—and because I am hidden in You, I will not be shaken either. I cancel the effects of every demonic interference designed to penetrate my defenses. No plan of the enemy will prevail tonight.

I declare divine closure to every residual chaos of this day. I shut the door to disaster. I bolt the windows to fear. I close every portal that would give the enemy access to torment me in the night. You are the God in the midst of me, and I shall not be moved.

I sleep knowing my life is locked inside the stronghold of Your presence. Trouble may knock, but it will not enter. Storms may rise, but I remain in peace. You are my very present help, and under Your watch, I rest safe and sound.

In Jesus' name, Amen.

SHIELD

UNSHAKABLE CONFIDENCE

> He alone is my rock and my salvation, my fortress. I will not be shaken.
> —Psalms 62:6 WEB

Mighty Fortress, You alone are my rock and my salvation. You are my defense—I shall not be moved. Tonight, I lift the shield of confidence in You. I do not rely on the strength of flesh or the fleeting stability of circumstances. My safety is not tied to calm surroundings but to the God who stands guard over me. You are the rock beneath me and the wall around me.

Shield me, Lord, from the tremors of fear and the arrows of anxiety. Cover my mind from torment and my heart from heaviness. Let the fiery darts of doubt fizzle out in the presence of Your truth. Let every emotional aftershock from today dissolve in the stillness of Your strength.

I am held in place by a God who cannot be shaken. The winds may howl, and the shadows may deepen, but I remain grounded—shielded by the assurance that You are with me, for me, and around me.

Tonight, I rest—not just in safety, but in supernatural confidence.

In Jesus' name, Amen.

SILENCE

NO WISDOM CAN PREVAIL

> There is no wisdom nor understanding nor counsel against Yahweh.
> —Proverbs 21:30 WEB

Sovereign Lord, Your Word declares that there is no wisdom, no insight, and no plan that can succeed against You. So tonight, I silence every voice rooted in false wisdom, manipulation, or fear. I take authority over every counsel of darkness and every whisper of deception. I declare: if it doesn't come from You, it has no power over me.

Let every demonic strategy be overturned. Let every lying voice in my mind be dismissed by the voice of truth. I silence the accuser. I muzzle the tormentor. I still the inner critic and cancel every counterfeit revelation that tries to take root in the quiet of night.

You alone are wise. Your counsel stands forever. So I bring my thoughts into alignment with heaven's verdict: I am chosen, covered, and kept. I will not lose sleep over lies. I will not entertain whispers that contradict Your Word.

Tonight, every plan that is not of You is rendered void. I fall asleep under the rule of divine wisdom—and nothing else.

In Jesus' name, Amen.

Show

Taught by the Spirit

> But the Counselor, the Holy Spirit, whom the Father will send in my name, he will teach you all things, and will remind you of all that I said to you.
> —John 14:26 WEB

Holy Spirit, my Comforter and Teacher, I yield myself to Your instruction tonight. Even as my body rests, let my spirit remain attentive to what You want to reveal. You do not slumber, and You never stop speaking. So in the stillness of night, teach me again. Bring to remembrance every truth I've forgotten and uncover insights I've yet to see.

Let this night be a classroom of divine understanding. Let dreams carry wisdom. Let visions unveil direction. Bring back to mind Scriptures I've read, words You've spoken, promises I've doubted. Let light flood the rooms of my heart where confusion once lingered.

Tonight, I trade restlessness for revelation. I am not just closing my eyes—I'm opening my spirit. Teach me what I need for tomorrow. Remind me of what I've missed. Show me what I must embrace and what I must release.

You are my Teacher, and I trust Your gentle instruction even in the night hours. As I sleep, speak. As I rest, reveal.

In Jesus' name, Amen.

SLEEP

DARKNESS IS NOT DARK TO YOU

> If I say, "Surely the darkness will overwhelm me; the light around me will be night;" even the darkness doesn't hide from you, but the night shines as the day. The darkness is like light to you.
> —Psalms 139:11-12 WEB

Omnipresent Father, even if the darkness surrounds me, it is not dark to You. The night shines like the day in Your presence. I rest tonight with the full assurance that no shadow can hide me from Your sight. I am never out of reach. Never forgotten. Never unseen.

Let Your light shine through every hidden fear and unspoken worry. Illuminate the corners of my soul where I've buried concern. As I sleep, let the warmth of Your presence wrap around me and banish every lie that says I'm alone in the dark. I'm not. You are with me here. Your Spirit hovers even now.

There is no fear in this darkness, because You've filled it with Yourself. I lie down not in gloom, but in glory. I breathe in peace and exhale trust. Let Your nearness be more real than the silence, more present than the shadows, more powerful than the unknown.

I will rest deeply tonight, because the dark cannot hide me from You. I am safe in the night—and even safer in Your light.

In Jesus' name, Amen.

DAY 27

SHUT

AFFLICTION SHALL NOT RISE AGAIN

What do you plot against Yahweh? He will make a full end.
Affliction won't rise up the second time.
—Nahum 1:9 WEB

O Lord, the God who puts an end to trouble, I stand tonight on the promise that affliction will not rise a second time. I shut every gate to recurring battles and repeated cycles. I cancel every pattern of spiritual harassment and torment that seeks to revisit my life. What You have defeated shall not return. What You have broken will not be rebuilt. What You have buried in victory will not resurrect in defeat.

I declare that every open door to past pain, failure, oppression, or trauma is now sealed by the blood of Jesus. Let no familiar spirit gain access. Let no generational curse or demonic cycle break through the covering of Your covenant. I shut the door with faith and bolt it with finality.

Tonight, I sleep knowing I will not wake up to yesterday's war. I am free, I am protected, and I am moving forward with no backward steps. Let every monitoring spirit be blinded. Let every voice of intimidation be silenced. What was, shall not be again.

In Jesus' name, Amen.

SHIELD

You Are My Strong Tower

> For you have been a refuge for me, a strong tower from the enemy.
> —Psalms 61:3 WEB

Strong Tower and Shelter, I run to You tonight and find safety in Your heights. When my heart is overwhelmed, You lead me to a rock that is higher than my fear, higher than my confusion, higher than my limitations. You lift me above the reach of the enemy, where his weapons cannot touch me and his words cannot wound me. I am safe because You are strong.

Cover me in this hour, Lord. Shield me from every surprise attack, emotional ambush, or hidden trap laid in the dark. Let the fire of Your presence surround my home and my mind like a fortress. Guard the gate of my heart from despair. Guard the corridors of my mind from intrusive thoughts.

You are not only my defense—you are my dwelling. I remain in You tonight, wrapped in mercy, surrounded by peace, and fortified in faith. I rest under the shield of the unshakable God.

In Jesus' name, Amen.

SILENCE

BY THE BLOOD AND MY TESTIMONY

> They overcame him because of the Lamb's blood, and because of the word of their testimony. They didn't love their life, even to death.
> —Revelation 12:11 WEB

Victorious Lamb, I overcome the accuser tonight by the blood You shed and the word of my testimony. I silence every condemning voice, every tormenting lie, and every demonic whisper that rises to accuse me in the night. The blood of Jesus is against every tongue lifted in judgment. The enemy's arguments are overruled. His voice is silenced.

I testify that I am redeemed. I testify that I am covered. I testify that I am not under condemnation but under covenant. I declare that no accusation can stick, no shame can return, and no voice of fear can prevail over the voice of the blood.

Let the enemy's case be dismissed. Let his influence be nullified. Let peace reign in the courtroom of my mind. I lay down tonight not under the weight of guilt, but under the freedom of grace. My testimony is victory, and the blood is my defense.

In Jesus' name, Amen.

Show

Wisdom, Knowledge, and Understanding

> Now as for these four youths, God gave them knowledge and skill in all learning and wisdom; and Daniel had understanding in all visions and dreams.
> —Daniel 1:17 WEB

Wise and Wonderful Counselor, I thank You that You are the giver of skill, intelligence, and understanding. Just as You poured knowledge into Daniel and his friends, I ask tonight for divine insight to be deposited into my spirit as I rest. Let this be a night of mental clarity and spiritual enlightenment.

Teach me beyond textbooks. Guide me beyond logic. Unfold mysteries, strategies, and revelations that will position me for what's ahead. Give me understanding in dreams, vision in the night, and discernment that defies natural comprehension.

I am not limited to earthly wisdom—I receive the mind of Christ. Let this night be filled with instruction from heaven. Let the Spirit of wisdom and revelation rest upon me. I sleep not in ignorance but in the anticipation of divine downloads.

In Jesus' name, Amen.

Sleep

The Lord Sustains the Weary

> Yahweh opens the eyes of the blind. Yahweh raises up those who are bowed down. Yahweh loves the righteous. Yahweh preserves the foreigners. He upholds the fatherless and widow, but the way of the wicked he turns upside down.
> —Psalms 146:8-9 WEB

Compassionate God, You lift up those who are bowed down and sustain the fatherless and the oppressed. I come to You tonight in need of Your sustaining power. The day has worn me down, but You raise me up. My vision may be dim, but You open the eyes of the blind. My strength may feel gone, but You breathe life back into the weary.

As I lie down, I ask You to restore every depleted part of me. Let Your compassion reach into the deep places of my fatigue. Let Your hand support me through the night, cradling me in comfort. You do not sleep or slumber, so I don't need to carry the burdens of the world on my shoulders. I release them to You.

Tonight, I rest not as one abandoned, but as one upheld. I sleep under the eyes of a God who watches the vulnerable and lifts the broken. You are the God who sees me, shields me, and sustains me.

In Jesus' name, Amen.

DAY 28

SHUT

MY REFUGE IN TIMES OF TROUBLE

> Yahweh will also be a high tower for the oppressed; a high tower in times of trouble. Those who know your name will put their trust in you, for you, Yahweh, have not forsaken those who seek you.
> —Psalms 9:9-10 WEB

O Lord, my Refuge and my Stronghold, I shut the gates tonight to every trouble that tried to linger past its time. I declare that the Lord is my dwelling place—my fortified hiding place in times of affliction and pressure. No burden shall cross the threshold of this night. No storm will be permitted to invade my rest. I seal off every access point the enemy would use to stir fear, anxiety, or confusion.

I shut the door to doubt and close the window to torment. I stand firm in the truth that You are a refuge for the oppressed—a stronghold in hard times. I call upon Your name and take shelter beneath Your presence. As I close my eyes, I do not enter into the night uncovered—I enter into the shelter of the Most High.

I trust You, Lord, and because I trust You, I will not be shaken. You know those who seek You, and tonight, I draw near. I am hidden, secure, and sealed in divine protection. In Jesus' name, Amen.

SHIELD

I LOVE YOU, O LORD, MY STRENGTH

For the Chief Musician. By David the servant of Yahweh, who spoke to Yahweh the words of this song in the day that Yahweh delivered him from the hand of all his enemies, and from the hand of Saul. He said, I love you, Yahweh, my strength. Yahweh is my rock, my fortress, and my deliverer; my God, my rock, in whom I take refuge; my shield, and the horn of my salvation, my high tower.
—Psalms 18:1-2 WEB

Mighty Deliverer, I lift my voice to declare: I love You, O Lord, my strength. You are my rock, my fortress, and my shield. Tonight, I do not fight to protect myself—I lean into Your power and let You defend me. You are my covering and my escape, my stronghold and my song.

Wrap me in Your strength. Let every dart of discouragement be extinguished before it reaches me. Let every spirit of weariness and despair break against the shield of Your joy and power. I refuse to be vulnerable to the attacks of the night. My faith is not frail—it is anchored in the One who has never lost a battle.

You are not only near—you are active. So I lie down in confidence, not in fear. I rest knowing You are fighting for me even as I sleep. I love You, Lord—and in that love, I am protected.

In Jesus' name, Amen.

Silence

Quietness and Trust Will Be My Strength

> For thus said the Lord Yahweh, the Holy One of Israel, "You will be saved in returning and rest. Your strength will be in quietness and in confidence." You refused,
> —Isaiah 30:15 WEB

Holy Father, in repentance and rest is my salvation; in quietness and trust is my strength. So tonight, I release the need to strive. I surrender the urge to control. I quiet my soul before You and silence the inner noise that fights for dominance. I cast down worry, I dismiss fear, and I command stillness to take root within me.

I will not let the noise of this world disturb the sanctuary of my rest. I silence the voice of pressure. I mute the voice of condemnation. I block the voice of distraction. In this holy hush, I remember that You are God—and You are enough.

Let peace rise where panic once reigned. Let calm flood where chaos once crept. In this stillness, I am strengthened. In this silence, I am shielded. In trust, I find new power to stand.

Tonight, I rest, not because everything is resolved—but because everything is surrendered.

In Jesus' name, Amen.

Show

You Will Seek Me and Find Me

> You shall seek me, and find me, when you search for me with all your heart. I will be found by you," says Yahweh, "and I will turn again your captivity, and I will gather you from all the nations, and from all the places where I have driven you, says Yahweh. I will bring you again to the place from where I caused you to be carried away captive."
> —Jeremiah 29:13-14 WEB

God who draws near, You promised that when I seek You with all my heart, I will find You—and You will be found by me. So tonight, I seek You in the stillness of the night. Let this be more than sleep—let it be sacred searching. Come near to me in dreams, in whispers, and in revelation.

Let every question I've carried today find holy answers as I rest. Let hidden things be unveiled. Let divine direction surface in the silence. Let my hunger lead me into encounter. I don't want to settle for surface-level faith—I want to know You deeply, truly, intimately.

Tonight, I reach out with expectation. Meet me in the midnight moment. I trust that even as I lie still, You are drawing me into truth, showing me the way, and flooding me with Your presence.

In Jesus' name, Amen.

Sleep

He Will Quiet Me With His Love

> Yahweh, your God, is among you, a mighty one who will save. He will rejoice over you with joy. He will calm you in his love. He will rejoice over you with singing.
> —Zephaniah 3:17 WEB

Father of Compassion, thank You for singing over me with joy and quieting me with Your love. Let that love cover me now—let it hush every anxious voice and cradle me into calm. I am not alone in this night. I am not forgotten in this silence. You are here, closer than breath, speaking love into every part of me that feels restless or weary.

Quiet my heart, Lord, like a child safely nestled in a parent's arms. Let every internal storm be calmed by Your nearness. I breathe deeply now, letting the weight of Your affection press gently on every burden I've carried. Your love is not passive—it's powerful. And tonight, it holds me together.

Let me fall asleep under the sound of Your delight. Let Your rejoicing silence the accusations, and let Your presence still the worry. I do not have to earn rest—I simply receive it as a gift from the One who loves me endlessly.

In Jesus' name, Amen.

DAY 29

SHUT

OPEN ONLY THE GATES OF RIGHTEOUSNESS

> Open to me the gates of righteousness. I will enter into them.
> I will give thanks to Yah.
> —Psalms 118:19 WEB

Righteous Father, I thank You tonight for the gates that You've opened and those You've shut. I come before You with a heart set apart, asking that You seal every access point to unrighteousness in my life. I shut the gates to sin, to deception, to temptation, and to unholy alliances. I declare that only the gates of righteousness will remain open before me tonight.

Lord, I will not entertain what You've condemned. I will not leave open spiritual doors to fear, compromise, or distraction. I enter only through the gate that leads to Your presence, and I shut every other way behind me. No intruder shall pass through. No enemy shall cross the threshold. I am enclosed, kept, and guarded by the narrow gate that leads to life.

Let Your truth be the lock, and let Your Spirit be the guard. I rest tonight under divine protection, with no open gate for the enemy to access.

In Jesus' name, Amen.

Shield

Let Your Mercy Always Surround Me

> Don't withhold your tender mercies from me, Yahweh. Let your loving kindness and your truth continually preserve me.
> —Psalms 40:11 WEB

Compassionate God, as I settle in for the night, I ask You to surround me with the covering of Your mercy. Let steadfast love and truth be my shield. Do not withhold from me Your tender mercies, Lord, but let them flow over me like a canopy as I sleep. Where I feel exposed, be my cover. Where I feel weary, be my strength.

I trust You to be my defender, not because I've earned it—but because You are good. Shield me from the accusations of the enemy and the echoes of yesterday's regrets. Let the voice of Your mercy speak louder than my failures and shield my mind from torment. I do not sleep as one condemned—I sleep as one covered by compassion.

Wrap me in the warmth of Your never-ending mercy. Let every fiery dart aimed at my soul be quenched by the flood of Your lovingkindness.

In Jesus' name, Amen.

SILENCE

THE LORD REIGNS
—LET EVERY OTHER VOICE BE STILL

> Say among the nations, "Yahweh reigns." The world is also established. It can't be moved. He will judge the peoples with equity.
> —Psalms 96:10 WEB

Lord of all, You reign. Your throne is established, unshaken, and eternal. So tonight, I silence every voice that speaks contrary to that truth. I command stillness over every internal storm and rebuke every external voice that challenges Your sovereignty in my life. Let the roar of fear, chaos, and control be stilled by the declaration: *The Lord reigns.*

I will not let the voices of the world dictate my rest. I will not let the voice of fear narrate my future. You are ruling, reigning, and resting—so I will do the same. You are not anxious, and neither shall I be. I silence the accusations, the distractions, and the torment.

Let Your Word be the final voice in my heart tonight. You reign in my mind, over my emotions, and within my atmosphere. Let every spiritual disturbance now submit to the dominion of Christ.

In Jesus' name, Amen.

Show

Light for the Next Step

NUN Your word is a lamp to my feet, and a light for my path.
—Psalms 119:105 WEB

Illuminating God, Your Word is a lamp to my feet and a light to my path. As I lie down tonight, I ask that You shine the light of revelation upon my next steps. Even when the road ahead feels uncertain, You never leave me in the dark. You are the God who speaks in the night and guides through the shadows.

Reveal what I need to see—about You, about me, and about the assignment ahead. Let dreams be full of light. Let wisdom break through the veil of confusion. Illuminate my decisions. Show me what to surrender, what to pursue, and what to ignore. I lean not on my own understanding; I lean into Your light.

Let my path be cleared by the radiance of Your truth. As I sleep, remove the fog from my spirit. Let clarity rise, and let my eyes see with fresh insight. I trust You to guide me, even in the dark.

In Jesus' name, Amen.

Sleep

Abounding in Hope and Rest

> Now may the God of hope fill you with all joy and peace in believing, that you may abound in hope, in the power of the Holy Spirit.
> —Romans 15:13 WEB

God of hope, fill me tonight with all joy and peace as I trust in You. Let me abound in hope by the power of the Holy Spirit. I lay down not in despair, but in confident expectation. You are working while I am resting. You are moving even as I am still. Let Your peace be the atmosphere of my room and Your presence the blanket around my soul.

I cast every care at Your feet and make room for joy to rise. Though the night may seem long, I know morning is coming. Though the world is restless, I rest in Your promises. I don't need all the answers to rest in Your arms. I simply believe You are enough.

Let joy return where sorrow has lingered. Let peace flow like a river through the quiet of my soul. Let hope flood every weary place and make space for supernatural renewal.

I sleep tonight full of hope, full of trust, and full of peace.

In Jesus' name, Amen.

DAY 30

SHUT

PRESERVE ME, O GOD

A Poem by David. Preserve me, God, for in you do I take refuge.
—Psalms 16:1 WEB

Preserving Father, I come into this final night of this journey declaring: *Preserve me, O God, for in You I take refuge.* I shut every gate to premature death, spiritual decay, and emotional breakdown. I will not end in loss, but in victory. I will not lie down vulnerable, but shielded by Your covenant to preserve my soul, my purpose, and my peace.

Every doorway the enemy has waited to enter—I now seal shut by the authority of Your name. Let no threat, no shadow, no arrow reach my dwelling. I will not be stalked by fear, chased by doubt, or haunted by weariness. I am enclosed by mercy and surrounded by fire.

Tonight, I lie down under divine preservation. You keep what I commit into Your hands. My rest is not careless—it is confident.

In Jesus' name, Amen.

Shield

I Will Trust and Not Be Afraid

> Behold, God is my salvation. I will trust, and will not be afraid; for Yah, Yahweh, is my strength and song; and he has become my salvation."
> —Isaiah 12:2 WEB

Faithful Deliverer, You are my salvation, my strength, and my song. Tonight, I declare—I will trust and not be afraid. Let Your shield of trust surround me on every side. When the voice of fear tries to rise, I speak back: *Behold, God is my salvation.* I rest beneath the confidence of Your love.

Shield my mind from worry about the unknown. Guard my heart from the lingering sting of disappointment. Let Your strength rise between me and every weakness. You are not only able to protect me—you delight to do so. Wrap me in the safety of covenant love.

As I surrender this day and all it held, I find myself cradled in divine assurance. I will not be afraid of the dark, of tomorrow, or of spiritual warfare. You are with me—and that changes everything.

In Jesus' name, Amen.

Silence

With a Sword in My Mouth

> May the high praises of God be in their mouths, and a two-edged sword in their hand; To execute vengeance on the nations, and punishments on the peoples;
> —Psalms 149:6-7 WEB

Warrior God, I rise tonight in the authority of Your Word. Let the high praises of God be in my mouth and a two-edged sword in my hand. I silence every opposing voice—not with fear, but with worship. Every tongue lifted against me in the night is silenced by the power of praise. Let the spirit of accusation be muzzled. Let every midnight plot be undone.

I will not sleep in defeat. I will lie down in triumph. I lift praise as a weapon and let Your justice move. Every dark agenda against my life is overturned. Every whisper in the night is drowned by my declaration: *God reigns, and I belong to Him.*

Let Your vengeance execute righteousness, and let the enemy know I am not without backup. The Lord of Hosts fights for me. His Word is in my mouth, and His fire is in my praise.

In Jesus' name, Amen.

SHOW

THE SPIRIT OF PROPHECY IS JESUS

> I fell down before his feet to worship him. He said to me, "Look! Don't do it! I am a fellow bondservant with you and with your brothers who hold the testimony of Jesus. Worship God, for the testimony of Jesus is the Spirit of Prophecy."
> —Revelation 19:10 WEB

Revealing God, I open myself tonight to the testimony of Jesus—the spirit of prophecy. As I rest, let my spirit hear what You are speaking. Let the dreams You give declare Your plans. Let the whispers in the night echo Your promises. I am not seeking signs—I am seeking You. And in seeking You, revelation flows.

Unlock the things to come. Let the testimony of Christ arise in clarity and fire. Show me my alignment in Your unfolding story. Reveal strategies, assignments, and encouragement that anchor my soul. I am not wandering—I am walking by Your light.

I listen not for entertainment, but for divine direction. Speak, Lord, for Your servant is listening. Reveal Jesus in deeper ways. Let the prophetic river flow even as I sleep, and let me awaken filled with vision.

In Jesus' name, Amen.

Sleep

There Shall Be No Night There

> There will be no night, and they need no lamp light; for the Lord God will illuminate them. They will reign forever and ever.
> —Revelation 22:5 WEB

Eternal Light, I thank You that even in the deepest night, You shine brighter than the sun. Tonight, I rest with the promise that there shall be no night where You dwell. So let the shadows flee from my spirit. Let the warmth of Your glory dispel every trace of heaviness. In You, the night holds no fear—only peace.

You are my lamp, my everlasting light. There is no need for artificial peace or temporary relief. You give rest that restores, sleep that heals, and comfort that lingers. As I lie down, let me taste of that eternal stillness, where the Lamb is the light and every tear is wiped away.

Let this be more than sleep—let it be sacred communion with the God who never grows weary and never leaves. I rest in eternal light, untouched by fear, wrapped in hope, and renewed by Your presence.

In Jesus' name, Amen.

Epilogue

You have just completed 30 nights of intentional prayer, prophetic declaration, and spiritual alignment. But this is more than the end of a devotional journey—it is the beginning of a new rhythm. You've learned to close your day not with chaos or passivity, but with purpose, peace, and power.

Every night, you have shut the gates of darkness, refusing access to fear, oppression, and spiritual intrusion. You have stood under the shield of God's wings, declaring divine protection over your body, your home, and your mind. You have silenced the midnight voices, rebuking every lie and tuning your spirit to the truth of God's Word. You have cried out, "Show me Your ways, O Lord," and invited divine revelation, dreams, and instruction into your night watches. And finally, you have rested with the confidence to say, "I lie down and sleep in victory," trusting that the God who watches over you neither slumbers nor sleeps.

These aren't just prayers—they are habits of dominion. You have built an altar at night and taken back sacred ground. And as you continue this lifestyle of evening command, expect to see long-term transformation—in your sleep, in your mind, in your spirit, and in your future.

Now, carry this practice with you. Continue to command your night, and let every morning greet you with fresh mercy, renewed strength, and unstoppable peace. Your night is no longer unguarded. It is governed.

Sleep boldly. Rise in victory. Live with purpose.

ENCOURAGE OTHERS WITH YOUR STORY

If this prayer guide has strengthened your faith, deepened your intercession, or helped you stand in the gap for our nation, would you consider leaving a short review on Amazon? Your feedback not only encourages others but also helps more believers discover this resource and join in the prayer movement. Every review—just a few sentences—makes a difference and helps spread the call to command the night. Thank you for being part of this movement.

More from PrayerScripts

Command Your Morning: 30 Days of Prayers and Declarations to Seize Your Day and Shape Your Destiny

---

There is a battle over every morning—and every believer must choose to either drift into the day or command it.

Command Your Morning: 30 Days of Prayers and Declarations to Seize Your Day and Shape Your Destiny is a spiritually charged guide to help you start each day with purpose, power, and prophetic clarity. This is more than a devotional—it's a call to action. Each day in this 30-day journey is built around **five core biblical themes** that set the spiritual tone for your day: **Praise, Purpose, Protection, Provision** and **Position.** Don't just wake up. Command your morning—and shape your destiny.

COMMAND YOUR EVENING: 30 DAYS OF PRAYERS AND DECLARATIONS TO RELEASE THE DAY AND RECLAIM INTIMACY WITH GOD

There is a battle over every transition—and evening is one of the most spiritually neglected.

Command Your Evening is the third book in the **Command Your Destiny** series—following *Command Your Morning* and *Command Your Night*. In heaven's rhythm, the evening is not just a wind-down—it's a window. A sacred hour where destinies are recalibrated, burdens are lifted, and hearts are re-centered in the presence of God. In *Command Your Evening*, you'll journey through 30 days of intentional, Spirit-led prayers and prophetic declarations centered around five key evening themes: **Release, Renew, Refocus, Rebuild,** and **Rest**.

STANDING IN THE GAP FOR COVENANT AWAKENING:

30 DAYS OF PRAYER FOR NATIONAL REPENTANCE, RIGHTEOUS LEADERSHIP & GOD'S SOVEREIGN RULE

What if your prayers could help turn the tide of a nation?

America stands at a spiritual crossroads. Division deepens, truth is under siege, and righteousness is being redefined. But God is still searching for those who will stand in the gap—intercessors who will cry out for mercy, justice, and national awakening.

Standing in the Gap for Covenant Awakening is a 30-day prayer guide for believers who sense the urgency of the hour and long to see their nation return to God.

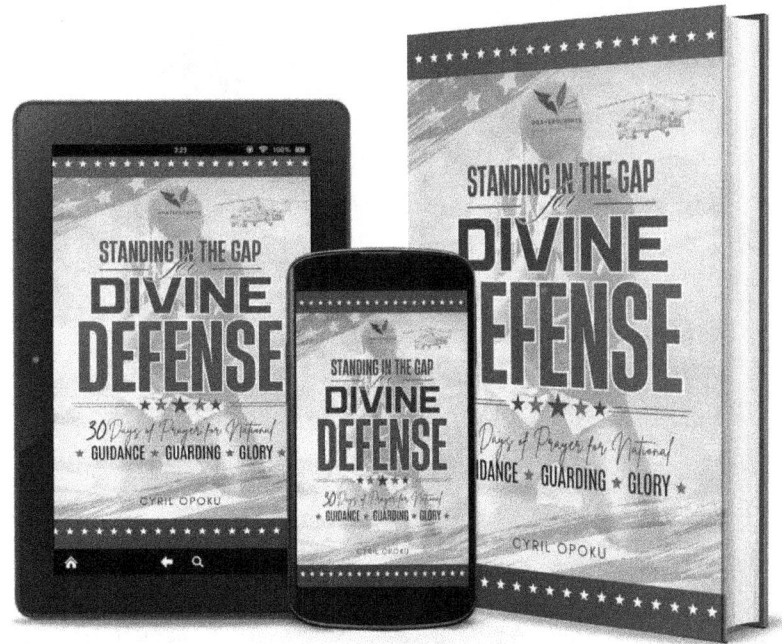

STANDING IN THE GAP FOR DIVINE DEFENSE:

30 DAYS OF PRAYER FOR NATIONAL GUIDANCE, GUARDING & GLORY

When the foundations of a nation feel as if they're shaking, prayer is the strongest fortress you can build.

Standing in the Gap for Divine Defense: 30 Days of Prayer for National Guidance, Guarding & Glory is your call to action—a 30-day journey of powerful, Scripture-rooted intercession that invites everyday believers to become watchmen on the walls for their nation. Drawing on timeless truths from God's Word, this devotional equips you to stand in the gap for your nation and **Seek Heaven's Wisdom, Secure Divine Protection,** and **Ignite Spiritual Awakening.** If you sense the urgency of the hour and long to see your country guided and guarded by the hand of God, open these pages. Stand in the gap. Watch Him move.

STANDING IN THE GAP FOR NATIONAL HEALING:

40 DAYS OF PRAYER FOR RECONCILIATION, RIGHTEOUSNESS, AND RESTORATION

What if your prayers could help heal a nation? What if God is waiting for someone—like you—to stand in the gap?

Standing in the Gap for National Healing: 40 Days of Prayer for Reconciliation, Righteousness, and Restoration is a bold, Spirit-filled call to action for believers who refuse to sit on the sidelines while their nation drifts further from God. In a time marked by division, confusion, and moral decline, this book equips you to pray with power, precision, and unshakable hope. Inside, you'll find 40 days of Scripture-based intercession divided into three strategic sections: **Peace, Unity & Reconciliation, Morality, Truth & Righteous Leadership,** and **National Restoration & Reformation.** It's time to stop watching history unfold—and start shaping it in prayer.

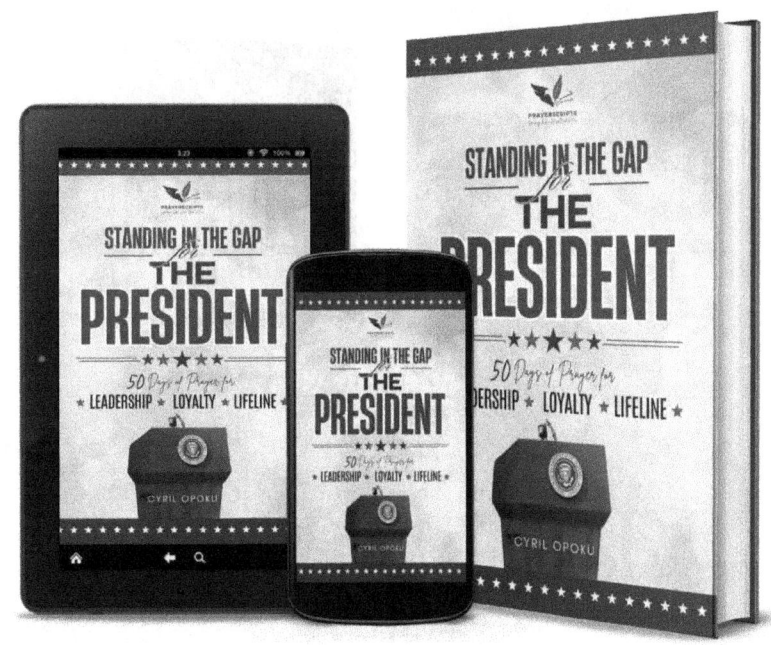

STANDING IN THE GAP FOR THE PRESIDENT:

50 DAYS OF PRAYER FOR LEADERSHIP, LOYALTY, AND LIFELINE

When a nation's leader is under spiritual siege, will you answer the call to stand in the gap?

Standing in the Gap for The President: 50 Days of Prayer for Leadership, Loyalty, and Lifeline is a bold, Scripture-saturated prayer guide for those who understand that the battles facing our leaders are more than political—they are spiritual. Assassination attempts, betrayal from within, and attacks on character and conscience are not just headlines—they're signs of the times. Inside, you'll find 50 days of strategic intercession divided into three high-impact sections: **Presidential Character & Leadership**, **Against Disloyal Insiders**, and **Against Assassination Attempts**. The future of a nation can shift through the prayers of the faithful. It's time to stand in the gap.

Scriptures & Prayers for Deliverance from Trouble:
40 Days of Prayer for When Life Feels Overwhelming

Are you walking through a season where life feels heavy, hope feels distant, and your prayers feel weak?

Scriptures & Prayers for Deliverance from Trouble is a 40-day journey of honest prayers and powerful Scriptures to help you find peace, strength, and healing when life is overwhelming. Each day offers a personal, Scripture-based prayer written in the language of real faith and raw trust. This devotional isn't about perfect words—it's about real connection with God when you need Him most.

Scriptures & Prayers for Deliverance from Evil:

50 Days of Prayer to Overcome Darkness and Find God's Protection

When darkness presses in, how do you pray?

When fear grips your heart or unseen battles rage around you, you need more than generic words—you need Scripture, truth, and the steady hand of God to lead you through.

Scriptures & Prayers for Deliverance from Evil: 50 Days of Prayer to Overcome Darkness and Find God's Protection is a powerful devotional journey designed to help you pray boldly and biblically through seasons of spiritual warfare, oppression, fear, or uncertainty.

SCRIPTURES & PRAYERS FOR ENGAGING THE ENEMY:
70 DAYS OF PRAYER TO REBUKE THE ENEMY AND RELEASE GOD'S POWER

You weren't called to run from the battle—
you were anointed to win it.

Scriptures & Prayers for Engaging the Enemy: 70 Days of Prayer to Rebuke the Enemy and Release God's Power is a bold devotional for believers who are ready to rise, resist, and reclaim what the enemy has tried to steal. If you're tired of feeling spiritually outnumbered, this book will equip you to fight back—with Scripture in your mouth and power in your prayers. Over 70 days, you'll be guided through five strategic phases of spiritual warfare: (1) Rebuking the Enemy, (2) Releasing Terror Upon the Enemy (3) Praying for the Fall of the Enemy (4) Treading Upon the Enemy (5) When Heaven Strikes.

The war is real. But so is your victory.

SCRIPTURES & PRAYERS FOR COMBATING SPIRITUAL WICKEDNESS:
50 DAYS OF PRAYER TO OVERTHROW WICKED PLANS AND STAND IN GOD'S VICTORY

Are you facing opposition that feels deeper than the natural? Do you sense hidden resistance working against your progress, peace, or purpose? You're not imagining it—and you're not powerless.

Rooted in the authority of Scripture and fueled by bold, targeted prayers, *Scriptures & Prayers for Combating Spiritual Wickedness* equips you to confront darkness head-on. Each day features a focused Bible passage and a heartfelt, Scripture-based prayer designed to nullify ungodly counsel, disrupt demonic schemes, and establish God's victory in every area of your life.

www.ingramcontent.com/pod-product-compliance
Lightning Source LLC
Chambersburg PA
CBHW050636160426
43194CB00010B/1693